The

Instant

Sewing Handbook

---

by WENDY RYDELL

Published by
CAREER INSTITUTE
555 East Lange Street   Mundelein, Illinois   60060

Instant Sewing Handbook

A quick reference guide for the home sewer

Copyright © 1972 by Career Institute, Inc.
Library of Congress Catalog Card No. 72-89526
Printed in the United States of America

ISBN 0-911744-12-6

IS 73-1

Contents

Introduction

So You're a Sewer

Like you, millions and millions of American women and girls sew. Why? Their reasons are as varied as the clothes they create, but these are among the most important. They sew because:

- They enjoy wearing the latest styles.

- They're long on fashion sense and short on clothing money.

- They have special figure problems that make buying ready-to-wear clothes difficult at best.

- They can sew a complete dress tonight—and wear it tomorrow.

- They can wear the "look" they like, whether or not it is available in the stores.

- They enjoy the sense of accomplishment that comes from an admiring glance and a sometimes-envious "And you made it *yourself!*"

- They are, above all, creative people.

The purpose of this book is to help you sew more quickly, more skillfully, more effectively, by presenting the major problems a home sewer faces—and offering a series of professional solutions.

It can be used by beginning and advanced sewers alike as an overview of the world of home fashion—or as an instant, easy-to-use reference to solve specific sewing problems

Most of all, it has been written to help you reach your own personal sewing goals.

Good sewing!

Wendy Rydell

CHAPTER 1

Put Yourself in the Fashion Picture

The Exciting World of Fashion

Women everywhere in the world like to look their best. Good health habits help; so does a well-balanced diet; so does the skillful application of makeup and an inner feeling of confidence.

But most of all, a woman feels her best when she is sure she is well dressed. And that is what fashion—good fashion —is all about.

Each season brings a wealth of new styles. Some are good; others are faddish, designed only for the handful of women who look like the models in high-fashion magazines.

The truly fashionable woman picks and chooses among the current styles, wearing those that are becoming to her and adapting others until they *are* becoming.

Her constant guide in clothing selection is the question "Will it look good on me?" If the answer is yes, the next question is "Will it fit into my way of life?"

The fashionable woman unerringly answers each question correctly. She unerringly selects those styles that work well for her—and for her unique needs. That is why she is always tastefully dressed. That is why she is a fashionable woman.

Her secret? She has discovered her own best fashion image. And so can you.

Fashioning Your Own Image

Fashioning your individual image begins with a good, hard look at yourself in a mirror. Appraise yourself carefully—and honestly. Are you a shade too short? Too tall? A little too thin? A little too broad?

Are you the sweet type? The sophisticated type? The outdoor-girl type?

What about your coloring? Is your complexion on the sallow side? Is it a bit too ruddy? Do you look and feel "washed out" in certain colors?

Make a list of each of the features you'd like to change. And don't forget to include a list of your good features, too, like a small waist, or long, graceful legs, or a very pretty face, or excellent posture.

Is the list of "changeables" longer than the list of assets? Don't despair: your problems are shared by many women. And some of them are among the best-dressed, most fashionable women in the world.

Creating an Illusion

The well-dressed woman who wins all those admiring glances may have some of the same figure problems you do. But you'd never know it because she is an artist who creates a fashion illusion by manipulating the three prime elements of design—line, color, and texture.

The Illusion of Line

Look at the two rectangles on the opposite page. Both are the same size. Yet the one with the vertical line, on the left, looks taller; the other, with the horizontal line, looks wider.

What makes rectangle A look taller than rectangle B? The vertical line of A carries the eye upward and creates the illusion of height, while the horizontal line of B carries the eye from side to side and creates the illusion of width.

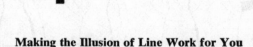

Making the Illusion of Line Work for You

Did your list of changeables include the words "too short?" You can create the illusion of height by choosing clothes with strong vertical lines.

Each of the illustrations shows how the use of strong vertical lines can add inches—and, suddenly, you're taller!

What happens if you'd rather whittle away a few inches? Using the same illusion of line, you can choose any of these techniques—and, suddenly, you're shorter!

The Illusion of Color

Color, like line, can play tricks on the eye. Prove it yourself by clipping out two squares of colored paper. Make each square the same size, but cut one of a warm color like yellow or orange and the other of a cool color like dark blue or green.

Which square looks larger? The warm one. Here's why.

Although there are hundreds of colors—warm and cool, bright and dull, light and dark—they are all derived from the three basic, or primary, colors: red, yellow, and blue.

Red and yellow and the entire range of colors between them are called warm colors. But when red or yellow is

4

mixed with blue, the cool color, the resulting colors are called cool colors.

Making the Illusion of Color Work for You

Remember your little experiment with the two squares of color paper—how the warm color made one square appear larger than the cool-colored square? The same principle applies to clothing colors.

Want to Look Smaller?   ### Want to Look Larger?

Wear a cool color.

Wear a dull or grayed color.   **Wear a warm color.**

Wear a dark color.   **Wear a bright color.**

          Wear a light color.

Compounding the Color Problem

What do you do if you are medium-tall, with thin hips and a rather heavy bust? Or the other way around?

Follow the same basic principles of creating a color illusion—and make color work for you.

A dress or ensemble with a cool, dark top and a warm, light skirt can visually move inches from the bust and add them to the hips. Reverse the colors and you can reverse the inches—visually, at least.

Color in the hands of a fashionable woman is much like a painter's palette in the hands of a talented artist. You can be that fashionable woman by making color work for you.

Would you like to highlight a graceful pair of legs or a slender, shapely neck? The clever use of a light, bright color accent at hemline or neckline can accomplish just such magic.

The Illusion of Texture

Today's modern fabrics come in many textures, from clingy, gossamer sheers to heavy, elegant brocades. Yet each fabric will react in its own special way to light, to shade, to movement; each fabric plays an important part in helping you create an illusion.

A lustrous fabric, like satin, will reflect light and visually add inches to the figure. A fabric with a dull finish will absorb light and visually subtract inches.

A clingy fabric, like jersey, will follow every contour of the body and exaggerate even the slightest figure flaw. A fabric with more body will conceal figure flaws, but a very stiff fabric, while concealing effectively, tends to broaden the overall silhouette.

Bulky fabrics, like heavy tweeds, may conceal a figure flaw but they seem to add inches in direct proportion to their bulkiness.

Making the Illusion of Texture Work for You

Fashionable clothes result in the perfect marriage of pattern and fabric. And the marriage is made more lasting when you consider your own figure in relation to both pattern and fabric.

The very thin woman who'd love to add a few visual inches might consider making a skirt out of a beautiful but bulky wool tweed; the woman who'd rather lose inches would make the same skirt out of a softer, less bulky wool.

The very thin woman might look marvelous in a shiny satin jump suit; the heavier woman selects a fabric that absorbs light.

Once again, the key to successful texture illusion is knowing what characteristics individual fabrics have—and choosing the ones that best solve your own particular figure problems.

Line, Color, Texture—Summing Up

There you are, reflected in the mirror, with your good and bad features staring back at you. And somewhere in your mind is the image of what you would like to be.

The tools for creating the newer, more fashionable you are line, color, and texture. Check the following chart for ways to put those tools to work.

7

Figure Problem	Dos	Don'ts
Too short	**Line:** strong verticals, long, fitted sleeves, narrow, self-fabric belts. **Color:** cool colors, light colors, depending on other figure problems. **Texture:** light- to medium-weight fabrics, small-patterned prints.	**Avoid** wide belts, very full skirts, strong horizontal lines, peplums. **Avoid** sharp color contrasts, two-color costumes in which color is divided equally. **Avoid** stiff or bulky fabrics.

TOO SHORT

TOO TALL

Too tall	**Line:** strong horizontals, skirts with fullness, peplums, tunics, wide, contrasting belts, short capes and jackets.	**Avoid** sheaths, strong vertical lines, V necks.
	Color: cool colors, dark colors, grayed colors, color contrasts between skirt and bodice.	**Avoid** bright colors, one-color coordinates.
	Texture: fabrics with body, fabrics that absorb light, large-patterned prints.	**Avoid** clingy fabrics, fabrics that hang limply.
Too heavy	**Line:** strong verticals, asymmetricals, panel fronts, eased sheaths, modified princess styles.	**Avoid** strong horizontal lines, fussy bodices, full skirts.
	Color: cool colors, dark colors, grayed colors, color contrasts with strong vertical effect (like navy blue with lighter blue front panel).	**Avoid** bright colors, light colors, bold patterns.
	Texture: Color-absorbing textures, medium-weight textures with moderate body.	**Avoid** shiny fabrics, light-reflecting fabrics, bulky fabrics, clingy fabrics, stiff fabrics.

TOO HEAVY

Too thin

TOO THIN

Line: horizontals, skirts with fullness, gathered or smocked details on bodice, wide collars, boxy jackets.

Color: warm colors, bright colors, light colors.

Texture: light-reflecting fabrics, medium to bulky fabrics, shiny fabrics, stiff fabrics.

Avoid strong vertical lines, sheaths, slim skirts, V necks, tight sleeves.

Avoid cool colors, dark colors, grayed colors.

Avoid light-absorbing fabrics, unless heavily draped.

10

Check the preceding chart for major figure problems and their solutions. Check the following chart for specific figure problems.

	Dos	Don'ts
Small bust	Draped bodices, wide collars, decorative bodice details.	Very high or very low neckline, fitted bodice.
Large bust	Simple necklines, asymmetrical bodice closings, long or three-quarter sleeves.	Deep V necklines, fussy collars, neckline bows or ties.
Thick midriff	Boxy jackets, overblouses.	Fitted-midriff styles.

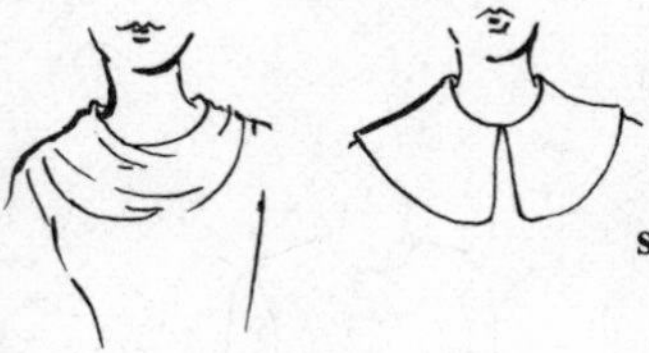

SMALL BUST

LARGE BUST

THICK MIDRIFF

| Short-waisted | Hip-length jackets, overblouses, long, smooth lines. | Contrasting belts, very slim or very full skirts. |
| Long-waisted | Wide belts and sashes, tunics, peplums, long jackets. | Too short shirts. |

SHORT WAISTED

LONG WAISTED

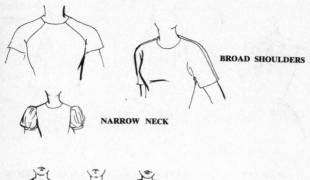

BROAD SHOULDERS

NARROW NECK

SHORT NECK

LONG NECK

Broad shoulders	Raglan sleeves, kimono sleeves.	Puffed sleeves, padded shoulders.
Narrow shoulders	Set-in sleeves with slight padding, puffed sleeves.	Raglan sleeves, dolman sleeves, kimono sleeves.
Short neck	V necklines, U necklines, small standaway collars.	Turtlenecks, high collars.
Long neck	Turtlenecks, mandarin necklines, high collars.	V necklines, U necklines, deep square necklines.

HIP HEAVY	**LARGE TUMMY**	**LARGE DERRIÈRE**

Hip heavy	Emphasize neckline and shoulders with interesting details.	Hip belts, sheath skirts, overblouses, tunics, peplums.
Large tummy	Emphasize sides of skirt or dress with shirring or pleats, leaving center panel straight.	Sheaths, sheath skirts, center-front details.
Large derrière	Hip-length boxy jackets, box-pleated skirts, gathered skirts.	Sheath skirts, back interest at waist or hipline.

Completing the Fashion Picture

You've followed the rules of line, color, and texture carefully. You've selected the right pattern, the right fabric. You've just finished a dress and you're delighted with the

14

results. But the handbag you thought to carry with your new dress isn't quite the right color. Or the shoes are a shade too dark. Or the coat you had planned to wear over it clashes with the color of the dress.

What went wrong? You forgot to color-coordinate your wardrobe.

Nothing stretches a closetful of clothes more completely, with less expenditure of money, than a properly-thought-out color coordination of each element.

Look at a color wheel and notice that colors directly opposite each other, complementary colors, go well with each other. And colors that adjoin each other blend very nicely together.

You have already selected those colors that work best for your figure and, of course, you've also considered them in relation to your own coloring.

Now—build your wardrobe around that basic color or colors by adding several secondary, or adjoining colors, and a complementary color for accents.

Example: your figure and coloring are ideal for a warm wardrobe—and you've chosen a warm, honeyed brown as your basic color. Thus:

Basic color—honey brown

Secondary colors—rust, camel, gold

Accents—orange, hot yellow, warm red

With this color scheme firmly in mind or, better still, written on paper, you might plan the following coordinated wardrobe:

Coat—honeyed brown

Jacket—camel

15

Skirts—brown/rust/gold plaid, orange/brown tweed, solid brown, solid red, solid camel.

Blouses—hot yellow, orange/gold/camel stripe, brown/rust/camel print, camel

Sweaters—orange, brown, gold

Dresses—red/brown print, gold/rust stripe, brown/orange plaid, solid brown, solid red, solid camel

Shoes—brown leather, rust suede

Handbags—brown leather, rust suede

Two things happen when you coordinate your wardrobe like this. One, you remember to follow your coordinated color scheme even for spur-of-the-moment purchases—belts, scarves, other accessories. Two, you can confidently combine any of the elements of your wardrobe and know that the overall affect will be flattering, color-correct—and fashionable.

Brown isn't your particular basic color? Then design your own best color scheme—the one best suited to your own figure and coloring.

You'll find that a half hour of color planning will save you disappointment—and an amazing amount of clothing dollars.

And now you're on your way to becoming the fashionable woman you've always wanted to be!

CHAPTER 2

Patterned for You

What's your favorite reading material? Magazines? Books? Newspapers?

The answer may be any or all of these. But, if you're a sewer, there is another kind of reading material that draws you like a magnet—a pattern book!

It's great fun to thumb through the pages of any commercial pattern book; to let your creative imagination run free; to visualize yourself in any one of the hundreds of styles illustrated.

And visualize you must—because, unlike a ready-made coat or dress or suit, there is no way a pattern can be tried on before you buy it to make sure it fits and flatters.

You have already learned many of the ways to flatter your own particular figure (see chapter 1). Here are the ways to guarantee that the patterns you select will fit you perfectly.

Pattern Size—the New Standard

Modern paper patterns are one of today's technical miracles. Every week, hundreds of thousands of patterns in a wide range of styles are sold to home sewers. And every Misses' Size 12, for example, is virtually the same size as every other Misses' Size 12.

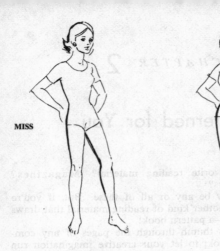

MISS

MISS PETITE

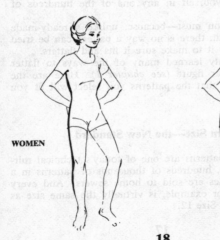

WOMEN

HALF SIZES

This tremendous degree of accuracy in standard pattern sizing has been developed deliberately by the major pattern companies to eliminate some of the guesswork in size selection.

But the human figure isn't standard—not by any means—so the pattern companies have developed a series of size ranges to conform to a variety of figure types.

Figuring Out Where You Fit

Today's patterns for girls and women are available in eight different size ranges for eight different figure types.

Misses'—designed for the "average" figure type: well-proportioned, well-developed figure about 5'5" to 5'6" without shoes, with normal waist length and bust position. *Size range: 6 to 18.*

Miss Petite—designed for the shorter "average" figure type: about 5'2" to 5'4" without shoes. *Size range: 6mp to 16mp.*

Women's—designed for the large, more mature figure type: about 5'5" to 5'6" without shoes, with normal waist length and bust position. *Size range: 38 to 50.*

Half-Size—designed for the shorter, fully developed figure type: about 5'2" to 5'3" without shoes, with short waist length. Waist and hips are larger in proportion to bust than in Misses' and Women's sizes. *Size range: 10½ to 24½.*

Junior—designed for the well-proportioned, short-waisted figure type: about 5'4" to 5'5" without shoes. Bust position is slightly higher than in Misses' sizes. *Size range: 5 to 15.*

JUNIOR

JUNIOR PETITE

YOUNG JUNIOR TEEN

GIRLS

Junior Petite—designed for the well-proportioned, petite figure type: about 5'0" to 5'1" without shoes, with shorter waist length and larger bust than in Junior sizes.
Size range: 3JP to 13JP.

Young Junior Teen—designed for the developed pre-teen and teen figure type: about 5'1" to 5'3" without shoes.
Size range: 5/6 to 15/16.

Girls'—designed for the underdeveloped figure type: about 5'0" tall without shoes.
Size range: 7 to 14.

Note: Since November 1, 1967, all major pattern companies have adopted new pattern sizing to correspond more closely to ready-to-wear sizes.

Figure-Typing Yourself

Now you're ready to see how you measure up to the eight standard size ranges and figure types established by the Measurement Standard Committee of the Pattern Fashion Industry.

The measurements you are about to take will be the key to perfect fit, so be sure they are taken carefully, accurately, and, if your figure changes, often.

The following suggestions and measurement charts will help to guarantee accuracy.

1. For best results, always have someone else do the measuring.

2. Wear the foundation garments you intend to wear under your new fashions.

3. Wear a slip or a close-fitting one-piece leotard over your undergarments—nothing more.

4. Tie a string or cord around your natural waistline.

5. Stand in stocking feet in your normal posture.

6. Keep a pencil handy to jot down each measurement as it is taken.

Your Fashion Measurement Chart

	Actual Measure-ment	Pattern Measure-ment	Alteration Needed (+ or —)
HEIGHT			
BUST			
WAIST			
HIPS 7" below waist			
HIPS 9" below waist			
ACROSS BACK armhole to armhole			
ACROSS UPPER CHEST			
SHOULDER TO WAIST front			
SHOULDER TO WAIST back			
CENTER FRONT from base of neck to waist			
CENTER BACK from base of neck to waist			
SHOULDER TO POINT OF BUST			
POINT OF BUST TO WAIST			
CENTER FRONT SKIRT LENGTH			
CENTER BACK SKIRT LENGTH			

22

SLEEVE LENGTH with arm
  slightly bent
    TO ELBOW
    TO WRIST
UPPER ARM around
  heaviest part

IMPORTANT: Pattern measurements given for each size are based on standard body measurements, not on actual measurements of the pattern pieces. Each pattern company allows "ease"—an additional amount of room across bust, waist, hips, and back waist length so that the garment fits comfortably when you move. Ease usually allowed across bust is 3"; waist is ½" to 1"; hip is 1" to 2"; back waist length is ¼" to ½".

Taking Accurate Measurements

Measure HEIGHT by standing flat against a wall, marking the position of the top of your head. Measure from the floor up to mark and record your height in feet and inches.

Measure BUST by placing tape over the fullest part of the bust, under the arms and straight across the back.

Measure WAIST by placing tape snugly around your natural waistline.

Measure HIPS in two places, 7" below waist and 9" below waist, by placing tape around the hips.

Measure ACROSS BACK by placing tape straight across back from armhole to armhole, about 5" below the base of the neck.

Measure ACROSS UPPER CHEST by placing tape across the fullest part of the bust from armhole to armhole.

Measure SHOULDER TO WAIST front from top to shoulder across bust to waist.

Measure SHOULDER TO WAIST front from top of shoulder to back waist.

Measure CENTER FRONT from collarbone to waist.

Measure CENTER BACK from the most prominent vertebra at the back of the neck to back waist.

Measure SHOULDER TO POINT OF BUST from top of shoulder to the point of the bust.

Measure POINT OF BUST TO WAIST from point of the bust to waist front.

Measure CENTER FRONT SKIRT LENGTH from waist to

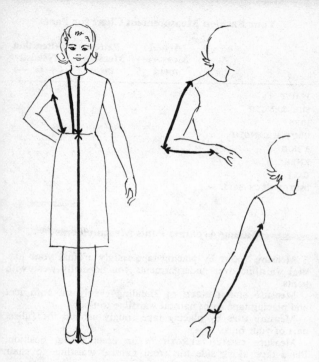

floor and subtract the number of inches skirt will be worn from floor.

Measure CENTER BACK SKIRT LENGTH from back waist to floor and subtract the number of inches skirt will be worn from floor.

Measure SLEEVE LENGTH from point of shoulder to both elbow and wrist with the arm slightly bent.

Measure UPPER ARM by placing tape around the heaviest part.

Your Fashion Measurement Chart for Pants

	Actual Measurement	Pattern Measurement	Alteration Needed (+ or —)
WAIST			
SIDE LENGTH			
HIPS			
CROTCH LENGTH			
THIGH			
KNEE			
CALF			
INSTEP PLUS HEEL			

Taking Accurate Pants Measurements

Measure WAIST by placing tape snugly around your natural waistline over undergarments you normally wear with pants.

Measure SIDE LENGTH by standing evenly on both feet and placing tape from natural waistline to floor.

Measure HIPS by placing tape snugly around the fullest part of your hips.

Measure CROTCH LENGTH in an erect sitting position. Place tape along side hip from natural waistline to chair and add ¾".

Measure THIGH by placing tape around the fullest part of your thigh near the crotch.

Measure KNEE by placing tape around the fullest part of knee.

Measure CALF by placing tape around the fullest part of the calf below the knee.

Measure INSTEP PLUS HEEL by placing tape across instep, below anklebone and around end of the heel.

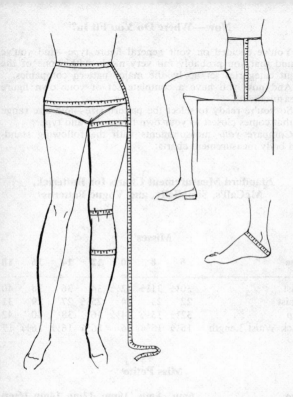

IMPORTANT: Remember that pattern manufacturers allow "ease"—an additional amount of room across waist and hips so that the garment fits comfortably when you move. Ease usually allowed across waist is ½" to 1"; hip is 1" to 2".

27

Now—Where Do You Fit In?

You've decided on your general figure type—and you've found that you probably fall very nicely within one of the eight categories set up by the major pattern companies.

And now you have a complete set of your own figure measurements.

So you're ready to select the pattern size—and size range —that comes closest to your own figure size and type.

Compare *your* measurements with the following standard body measurement charts:

Standard Measurement Charts for Butterick, McCall's, Simplicity, and Vogue Patterns

Misses'

Size	6	8	10	12	14	16	18
Bust	30½	31½	32½	34	36	38	40
Waist	22	23	24	25½	27	29	31
Hip	32½	33½	34½	36	38	40	42
Back Waist Length	15½	15¾	16	16¼	16½	16¾	17

Miss Petite

Size	6mp	8mp	10mp	12mp	14mp	16mp
Bust	30½	31½	32½	34	36	38
Waist	22½	23½	24½	26	27½	29½
Hip	32½	33½	34½	36	38	40
Back Waist Length	14½	14¾	15	15¼	15½	15¾

Women's

Size	38	40	42	44	46	48	50
Bust	42	44	46	48	50	52	54
Waist	34	36	38	40½	43	45½	48
Hip	44	46	48	50	52	54	56
Back Waist Length	17¼	17⅜	17½	17⅝	17¾	17⅞	18

Half-Size

Size	10½	12½	14½	16½	18½	20½	22½	24½
Bust	33	35	37	39	41	43	45	47
Waist	26	28	30	32	34	36½	39	41½
Hip	35	37	39	41	43	45½	48	50½
Back Waist Length	15	15¼	15½	15¾	15⅞	16	16⅛	16¼

Junior

Size	5	7	9	11	13	15
Bust	30	31	32	33½	35	37
Waist	21½	22½	23½	24½	26	28
Hip	32	33	34	35½	37	39
Back Waist Length	15	15¼	15½	15¾	16	16¼

Junior Petite

Size	3	5	7	9	11	13
Bust	30½	31	32	33	34	35
Waist	22	22½	23½	24½	25½	26½
Hip	31½	32	33	34	35	36
Back Waist Length	14	14¼	14½	14¾	15	15¼

Young Junior/Teen

Size	5/6	7/8	9/10	11/12	13/14	15/16
Bust	28	29	30½	32	33½	35
Waist	22	23	24	25	26	27
Hip	31	32	33½	35	36½	38
Back Waist Length	13½	14	14½	15	15⅜	15¾

Girls'

Size	7	8	10	12	14
Breast	26	27	28½	30	32
Waist	23	23½	24½	25½	26½
Hip	27	28	30	32	34
Back Waist Length	11½	12	12¾	13½	14¼

Measurement Charts for Spadea Patterns

Regular

Sizes	6	8	10	12	14	16	18	20
Bust	32	33	34	35	36½	38	40	42
Waist	22	23	24	25	26½	28	30	32
Hip (5" below waistline)	33	34	35	36	37½	39	41	43
Back Waist Length	16	16¼	16½	16¾	17	17¼	17½	17¾

For Mature Figures

Size	14	16	18	20	40	42	44
Bust	36½	38	40	42	44	46	48
Waist	27½	29	31	33	35	37	38
Hip (5" below waistline)	37½	39	41	43	45	47	49
Back Waist Length	17	17¼	17½	17¾	18	18¼	18½

For Short Figures 5'5" and Under

Size	8	10	12	14	16	18	20
Bust	33	34	35	36½	38	40	42
Waist	24	25	26	27½	29	31	33
Hip (5" below waistline)	34	35	36	37½	39	41	43
Back Waist Length	15¾	16	16¼	16½	16¾	17	17¼

For Tall Figures

Size	8	10	12	14	16	18	20
Bust	33	34	35	36½	38	40	42
Waist	23	24	25	26½	28	30	32
Hip (5" below waistline)	34	35	36	37½	39	41	43
Back Waist Length	17	17¼	17½	17¾	18	18¼	18½

For Half-Sizes

Size	12½	14½	16½	18½	20½	22½
Bust	35½	37½	39½	41½	43½	45½
Waist	27½	29½	31½	33½	35½	37½
Hip (5" below waistline)	35½	37½	39½	41½	43½	45½
Back Waist Length	15¾	16	16¼	16½	16¾	17

For Juniors

Size	5	7	9	11	13	15	17
Bust	31½	32½	33½	34½	36	37½	39
Waist	21½	22½	23½	24½	26	27½	29
Hip (5" below waistline)	32½	33½	34½	35½	37	38½	40
Back Waist Length	15½	15¾	16	16¼	16½	16¾	17

"But I Don't Quite Measure Up!"

You've read through the pattern measurement charts and compared them with your own—and you can't quite match all four key measurements.

Don't worry. Most women can't.

If you're one of the rare ones, you'll match all four measurements in a particular size. And, if you're very lucky, you may match three of the four.

But, if you're somewhere in the middle, choose the smaller size and enlarge the pattern *(see pages 46 to 75)* because it is much easier to make a pattern larger than smaller.

And, if there is a major difference between bodice and skirt measurements, it might be wisest to buy two patterns —one in the right size for the bodice and the other in the right size for the skirt—and alter both so they join properly at the waist.

It's What's on Top That Counts

Since the bodice of most dress patterns is most difficult to fit, it is wise to choose your dress pattern size according to bust measurement and make the necessary adjustments to the skirt.

As a general rule, skirt pattern size should be selected by waist measurement unless you hip measurement is two inches larger than the pattern hip measurement. Then, select according to hip measurement and alter the waist to fit. This same rule applies for shorts and slacks.

Proportioned Patterns

Some women find that they can match their measurements well enough in one of the standard size ranges, but their overall height—or lack of it—makes fitting difficult.

Today, many patterns are available in "proportioned

heights." These patterns are designed to fit tall (5'8" to 5'10"), average (5'6" to 5'7"), or short (5'3" to 5'5") figures.

All construction markings and proportioning details for each of the three heights are marked on every "proportioned" pattern.

Before You Make a Final Pattern Size Decision—

Look carefully at the silhouette chart below. Each silhouette is a Size 12—but that's where the similarity ends.

Find the silhouette that most closely resembles yours and follow these size suggestions:

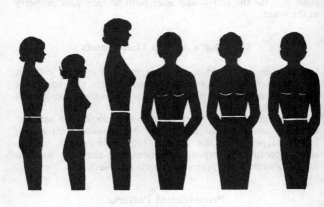

Size 12

AVERAGE should select Misses' Size 12.

SHORT should select proportioned Misses' Size 12, Miss

Petite Size 12, or Junior Size 11.

TALL should select proportioned Misses' Size 12 or standard Misses' Size 12 and lengthen both bodice and skirt.

WIDE SHOULDERS, NARROW HIPS should select Misses' Size 12 and widen bodice through the shoulders and narrow skirt through the hips.

LARGE HIPS, NARROW SHOULDERS should select Misses' Size 12 and widen skirt through the hips. If figure is particularly narrow through the bodice, it would be advisable to select Misses' Size 10 and enlarge skirt through the hips.

NARROW HIPS should select Misses' Size 12 and narrow skirt through the hips.

The next silhouette chart illustrates six different Size 40 figures. If this is your general size range, find the silhouette that most closely resembles yours and follow these size suggestions:

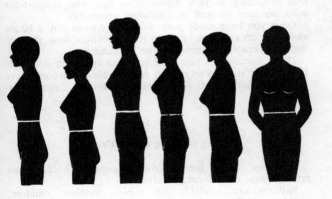

Size 40

AVERAGE should select Women's Size 40.

SHORT should consider selecting Half-Size 20½ if pattern alterations and reproportioning are major.

TALL should select Women's Size 40 and lengthen both bodice and skirt.

HIGH, LARGE BUST should select Women's Size 38 and adjust bustline in both width and length.

LOW BUST should select Women's Size 40 and lower underarm darts and enlarge through waist and hips if necessary.

NARROW HIPS should select Women's Size 40 and narrow the skirt through the hips.

And now, you're ready to make your pattern size selection according to your figure type, size, and proportions with the least amount of alteration necessary.

Once you have made your selection, do *not* buy a larger size for a coat or suit. Pattern manufacturers have allowed enough room for a lining and/or interlining.

If the pattern size you want is not in stock, do *not* settle for a larger size. Wait until it is available—and you'll save yourself major alterations and the possibility of a disappointing fit.

Fitting the Rest of the Family

Everyone in the family, from youngest to oldest, can proudly wear one of your creations.

Patterns are available for babies, toddlers, children, chubby girls, boys, teen-boys, and men.

However, to get the best fit, *Always buy by size, not by age.*

The following are standard body measurement charts for the rest of the family, along with the best method to take body measurements:

Babies

Age	Newborn (1 to 3 Months)	6 Months
Weight	7–13 lbs.	13–18 lbs.
Height	17"–24"	24"–26½"

These sizes are for infants who are not yet walking. Take weight and height of the infant. If weight and height fall into different sizes, make your size selection according to weight.

Toddlers'

Size	½	1	2	3	4
Breast or chest	19	20	21	22	23
Waist	19	19½	20	20½	21
Finished dress length	14"	15"	16"	17"	18"

These patterns are for toddlers—between baby and child. Toddler pants have a diaper allowance. Toddler dresses are shorter than a corresponding Children's size.

Take height measurement by standing child, without shoes, against a wall and measuring from the floor to the top of the head. Take breast or chest measurement under the arms with the tape over the fullest part of the chest in front and the bottom of the shoulder blades in back.

Children's

Size	1	2	3	4	5	6	6X
Breast or chest	20	21	22	23	24	25	25½
Waist	19½	20	20½	21	21½	22	22½
Hip	—	—	—	24	25	26	26½
Back waist length	8¼	8½	9	9½	10	10½	10¾
Approx. height	31"	34"	37"	40"	43"	46"	48"
Finished dress length	17"	18"	19"	20"	22"	24"	25"

Children's measurements are taken in the same way as Toddler measurements. The additional measurement, the hip, is taken around the fullest part of the hip. Back waist length is taken from the nape of the neck to the waist.

Chubbie

Size	8½c	10½c	12½c	14½c
Breast	30	31½	33	34½
Waist	28	29	30	31
Hip	33	34½	36	37½
Back waist length	12½	13¼	14	14¾
Approx. height	52"	56"	58½"	61"

These patterns are designed for the growing girl who is above the weight average for her age and height. These measurements are taken in the same way as toddler's or children's measurements.

Boys' and Teen-Boys'

Size	7	8	10	12	14	16	18	20
Chest	26	27	28	30	32	33½	35	36½
Waist	23	24	25	26	27	28	29	30
Hip (seat)	27	28	29½	31	32½	34	35½	37
Neck	11¾	12	12½	13	13½	14	14½	15
Height	48"	50"	54"	58"	61"	64"	66"	68"

These patterns are designed for growing boys and young men who have not yet reached their full adult size. Boys' and teen-boys' measurements are taken around the neck

plus ½″, around the fullest part of the chest, around the waist measured over a shirt but not trousers, and around the fullest part of the hip or seat. Sleeve length is measured from the back base of the neck along the shoulder to the wrist.

Men's

Size	34	36	38	40	42	44	46	48
Chest	34	36	38	40	42	44	46	48
Waist	28	30	32	34	36	39	42	44
Hip (seat)	35	37	39	41	43	45	47	49
Neck	14	14½	15	15½	16	16½	17	17½
Sleeve length	32	32	33	33	34	34	35	35

These patterns are designed for men of average build about 5'10" without shoes. Men's measurements are taken in the same way as boys' and teen-boys' measurements.

Note: Boys', teen-boys', and men's sizing has been modified recently. Always *check* the sizing on the back of the pattern envelope of the style you select *before* you buy the pattern.

CHAPTER 3

More about Patterns:
How to Read Them—How to
Alter Them

Almost everything you need to know about the new fashion you're going to make can be found on the pattern envelope.

So take a few extra minutes to study it carefully—and you'll find that those extra few minutes can pay off handsomely.

Picturing Yourself in the Pattern

By now, you know your "fashion" self quite well—your proper size and size range, the styles that will be most flattering to you, and just how skilled a sewer you really are:

Keep these things carefully in mind as you read the front of the pattern envelope.

SELECT the right size and size range—the one you've decided comes closest to your figure type and measurements.

SELECT the kind of style that will be most flattering for you. And then, of the several versions illustrated on the pattern envelope front, select the version you're planning to make.

SELECT a style that falls well within your sewing ability. If you're a beginner, stay away from elaborate collar, bodice, shoulder, or skirt details—at least until your budding talent grows. And, if you're an expert, the sky's the limit!

Any special features of the pattern you've chosen— "easy-to-sew" or "proportioned-to-size" or "jiffy"—are also listed on the pattern envelope front.

More Information on the Back

And now, to the back of the pattern envelope.

The *small line drawings,* complete with construction details, show back views of each of the fashion versions sketched on the front. In case some construction details are hidden, a full written description is also supplied.

The line drawings, plus the written description, should confirm the fact that the fashion you've chosen will be flattering and well *within* your sewing ability.

The *second set of line drawings* on the back of the pattern envelope shows the individual pattern pieces you'll be working with. Each pattern piece is identified so you can judge the amount of sewing—and length of time—needed to put this particular fashion together.

The *body measurement chart* should be used to confirm the pattern size you have selected.

The *yardage chart* lists the necessary amount of fabric for each size and each version of the pattern you have selected. These yardage requirements have been carefully checked by the pattern manufacturer and are your most accurate guide to the exact amount of fabric you'll need to buy.

Be careful to notice whether yardage requirements are *"Without Nap"* or *"With Nap."*

Pattern pieces can be laid in opposite directions, up and down, only on fabric *"Without Nap."* Fabric *"With Nap"* must be cut with *all* pattern pieces laid out in the same direction. Fabrics *"With Nap"* include velvet, velveteen, fleece, fake fur, satin, napped flannels, and one-way prints, designs, or weaves. For these fabrics, additional yardage should be purchased.

Plaids, stripes, and one-way designs that need to be matched will also require additional yardage.

To help you select a suitable fabric for your pattern, a section called *Suggested Fabrics* is also included on the back of the pattern envelope. Read it carefully—and make your fabric selections accordingly.

These suggested fabrics have been recommended by the pattern designer because their particular weight and body will work successfully with the design. Although you don't need to follow these suggestions slavishly—other fabrics of comparable weight and body will also work—they *will* help you to select a suitable fabric for your new fashion.

As the pattern designer suggests which fabrics *to* use, he may also suggest which fabrics *not* to use. Some designs are cut in such a way that they are not suitable for fabrics with diagonal weaves or prints, plaids, checks, or stripes. *Do* follow these suggestions carefully.

Lining, underlining, and notions you'll need to complete your new fashion are also listed on the back of the pattern envelope. And the efficient sewer has learned to make these purchases at the same time she buys her fabric. It's so much easier to match buttons, bindings, trims, zipper, and thread on the spot—and lots handier when you're in the middle of sewing, and don't need to dash out to the store to pick up a blue 12″ zipper or a package of red bias binding.

Summing Up

From the information listed on the back of the pattern envelope:

CONFIRM your pattern choice after checking the body measurement chart for correct size and checking the written and illustrated construction details.

SELECT the pattern version you plan to make and check the fabric requirements carefully.

SELECT a suitable fabric based on the Suggested Fabric recommendations.

CHECK to make sure your fabric selection is without nap —or increase the necessary yardage if it is with nap. Additional yardage will also be necessary to match plaids, stripes, or one-way designs.

SELECT matching linings and/or underlinings and notions as suggested.

COMPLETE your purchases and get ready to make an exciting new fashion!

Before You Begin—Pattern Alterations for Perfect Fit

By selecting your pattern carefully according to your own figure type and measurements, you have eliminated most major alterations.

But, because you are human and final pattern measurements have been calculated by computers, there will probably be *some* alterations to make on the pattern pieces.

If you are, miracle of miracles, that perfect fit, turn to the next chapter. But, if you aren't, read on—and see how you can guarantee a perfect fit *before* you put scissors to fabric.

The Tape Measure Tells the Story

It's time now to check your Fashion Measurement Chart dimensions (*see chapter 2, page 22*) against the dimensions allowed on each of your major pattern pieces. The last column—ALTERATION NEEDED (+ or −)—will tell you at a glance where you need to be concerned about altering.

You'll need:

- a tape measure
- tissue paper
- straight pins
- and, to assure completely accurate measurements, a lukewarm iron to press all pattern pieces flat.

Lay each major pattern piece out flat—waist front, waist back, skirt front, skirt back, sleeve—noting all areas that will *not* be part of the outside of the finished garment. These include seam allowances, darts, stitched pleats, and any other bits of construction detail.

Don't add these areas into your measurements but *do* remember to add the ease allowed across bust, waist, and hips and along back waist length. And remember to double your measurement figures when a pattern piece is marked "Cut on Fold."

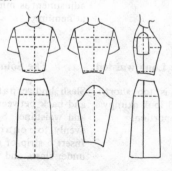

After you've completed your measurements of the pattern pieces and filled in the last two columns of your Fashion Measurement Chart, you know where you'll need to make alterations.

Is the pattern a bit too long? Too short? Is the waist too small? Too large? Are the hips too full? Too narrow?

There *is* an alteration solution for every figure problem. Simply check below to find your alteration problem—and its quickest, easiest solution.

The Problem: Short-waisted

The Solution

If the bodice is too long, it will fold over at the waistline.

Fold bodice pattern evenly across front and back between underarm and waistline until desired length is achieved.

If the skirt is too long, the fashion may look dowdy.

Fold skirt pattern evenly across front and back along hipline until desired length is achieved. Or, if length adjustment is minor, shorten at hemline.

The Problem: Long-waisted

The Solution

If the bodice is too short, the fashion will look skimpy and out of proportion.

Slash bodice pattern front and back between underarm and waistline. Spread apart evenly to required length. Insert a strip of tissue paper under slash, and pin.

If the skirt is too short, there is no way to lengthen it after cutting except by adding additional fabric and possibly unwanted seams.

Slash all skirt pattern sections straight across hipline. Spread apart evenly to required length. Insert a strip of tissue paper under slash, and pin.

Bustline Problems

The Problem: High Bust

Bodice fullness falls below fullest part of the bust, making bustline too tight and area below bust too full.

The Solution

For bust dart: Raise side bust dart, keeping it parallel to original dart. Raise point of waistline dart the same amount that bust dart was raised. Redraw pattern markings for both darts.

For French dart: Reposition pattern dart markings the required amount by drawing a line from center base of original dart to new position. Redraw dart markings to conform to new position.

The Problem: Low Bust

Bodice fullness falls above fullest part of bustline, making bustline too tight and area above bust too full and bunchy.

The Solution

For bust dart: Lower side bust dart, keeping it parallel to original dart. Lower point of waistline dart the same amount that bust dart was lowered. Redraw pattern markings for both darts.

For French dart: Reposition pattern dart markings the required amount by drawing a line from the center base of original dart to new position. Redraw dart markings to conform to new position.

HIGH BUST

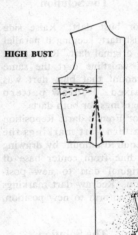

LOW BUST

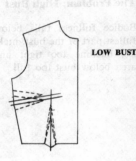

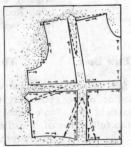

FULL BUST

The Problem: Full Bustline

Insufficient room across bustline causes pulling and wrinkling.

The Solution

Slash bodice front pattern through bust dart across front. Then slash pattern from shoulder over bustline through waistline dart. Spread pattern to desired length and width. Insert a strip of tissue under each slash, and pin. Additional width across shoulder and waistline can be taken in with darts.

For French dart: Slash on a straight line from center fold line of dart to center front. Spread pattern half the necessary amount, keeping neck edge on original center front. Insert a strip of tissue under slash and redraw dart lines to desired point.

The Problem: Small Bustline

Extra width across the bustline causes bunching and drooping.

The Solution

Draw a line through center of bust dart and center of waistline dart until the two lines meet. Continue line from this point to within ½″ of shoulder seam. Slash waist-to-shoulder line. Slash

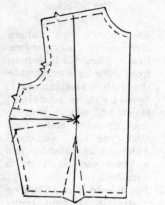

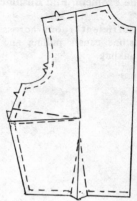

SMALL BUST

bust dart along line to within 1/8″ of point where the two lines met. Lap waist-to-shoulder slash the desired amount, and pin. This will automatically lap the bust dart slash, too. Pin.

For French dart: Slash on a straight line from center fold line of dart to center front. Lap slash half the necessary amount, keeping neck edge on original center front, and pin. Redraw dart lines from original stitch lines at base to desired point.

Shoulder Problems

The Problem:
Square Shoulders

Extremely square shoulders cause pulling and wrinkling across bust and shoulder blades up to shoulders.

The Solution

Lay bodice pattern front and back over tissue paper. Mark amount to be raised on tissue above armhole side seam. Redraw shoulder seam on tissue, meeting neckline. Pin. Mark the same increase above bodice side seam at armhole. Redraw seam line from mark to notches.

On a raglan sleeve: On original dart stitch lines, draw new stitch lines closer to edge and taper down to original dart point.

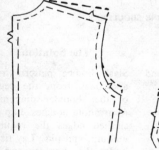

SQUARE SHOULDERS

The Problem:
Sloping Shoulders

The Solution

Fabric above bustline near arm seam droops and wrinkles.

Mark amount to be lowered along arm. Mark hole side seams on front and back bodices. Redraw shoulder seam lines from neckline to mark. Mark the same decrease on bodice side at armhole. Redraw seams from mark to notches.

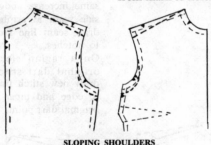

SLOPING SHOULDERS

The Problem:
Narrow Shoulders

The Solution

Seam line extends beyond the tip of the shoulder.

Slash bodice pattern front and back from the center of the shoulder diagonally to armhole notches. Lap the slashed edges the required amount, and pin. Lay tissue under the shoulder and redraw shoulder seam.

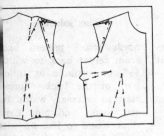

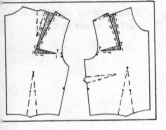

NARROW SHOULDERS

BROAD SHOULDERS

The Problem:
Broad Shoulders

Bodice pulls across shoulders from armhole to armhole.

The Solution

Slash bodice pattern front and back from the center of the shoulder parallel to armhole notches. Then slash from armhole notches to shoulder slash. Spread shoulder slash apart to necessary width. Insert a strip of tissue under slashes, and pin. Redraw shoulder seam to straighten.

The Problem: Round Shoulders

Bodice back pulls across shoulders and bunches at neckline.

The Solution

Slash across pattern bac from center back to withi ½" of armhole at fulle part of the back. Sprea slash to necessary width. I sert tissue, and pin. Co tinue tissue to line up wit original center back and fol excess along neckline into dart to retain size.

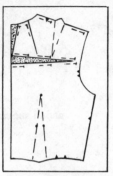

ROUND SHOULDERS

Neckline Problems

The Problem: Thin Neck

Neckline bunches and falls away from neck.

The Solution

Lay tissue under bodice pa tern front and back at neck line. Build up neckline th desired amount and redra neckline seam. Alter patter front and back facings th same amount and subtra that amount from bottom facings.

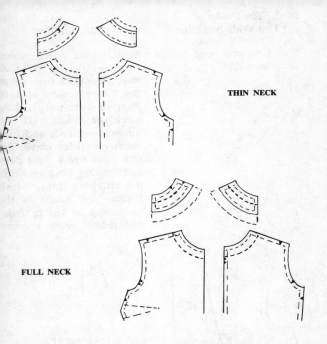

THIN NECK

FULL NECK

The Problem: Full Neck

Neckline pulls and wrinkles and is uncomfortably tight.

The Solution

Cut out neckline along front and back bodice patterns to desired size. Alter pattern front and back facings the same amount and add that amount to bottom of facings.

57

The Problem:
Too-Wide Neckline

The Solution

Neckline gaps and hangs away from neck.

Slash bodice front patter from neckline to point o bust. Then slash from waist line through center of wais dart to dart point. Lay neckline slash half th amount desired, and pin Redraw neckline curve. In sert tissue under waist dart and pin, but stitch on origi nal stitching lines. Slash bodice front facing in th same way as bodice from and redraw neckline curve

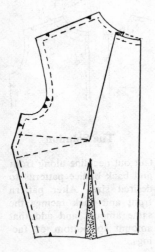

TOO WIDE NECKLINE

58

Back Problems

The Problem: Broad Back

Bodice pulls and stretches across back.

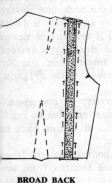

BROAD BACK

The Solution

Slash bodice back pattern from waistline to shoulder near armhole edge. Spread pattern to half the required amount. Insert tissue, and pin.

ERECT BACK

The Problem: Back Too Erect

Bodice back bags at waistline.

The Solution

Slash across bodice back pattern just above waistline to a point near the side seam. Lap slash the required amount, and pin, tapering to a point near the side seam. Redraw center back line to straighten.

Sleeve Problems

The Problem:
Large Upper Arm

The Solution

Sleeve pulls and wrinkles across upper arm.

Slash sleeve pattern on both sides from underarm toward center; then slash down toward lower part of sleeve. Spread slashes to desired width. Insert tissue, and pin. Redraw cap to original shape.

IMPORTANT: A corresponding alteration must be made in bodice front and back as follows:

Slash bodice pattern front and back sections from under arm toward waist. Spread slash to equivalent size. Insert tissue, and pin. Redraw armhole to original shape.

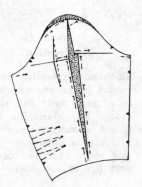

LARGE UPPER ARM

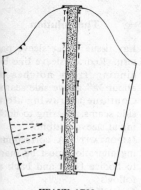

HEAVY ARM   **THIN ARM**

The Problem: Heavy Arm

Sleeve pulls and wrinkles at lower edge.

The Solution

Slash sleeve pattern through center from hemline to O pattern marking on cap. Spread the slash to the required size. Insert tissue, and pin.

The Problem: Thin Arm

Sleeve bunches over arm.

The Solution

Slash sleeve pattern through center from hemline to O pattern marking on cap. Lap slashed edges to decrease desired amount, and pin. Redraw hemline edge to straighten.

61

The Problem: Broad Shoulders

Sleeve pulls and wrinkles across top near shoulder.

The Solution

Lay tissue under sleeve pattern. Redraw sleeve line beginning from notches to about ⅜" above side seam. Continue redrawing along side seams, tapering to nothing at sleeve bottom.

IMPORTANT: A corresponding alteration must be made to bodice front and back as follows:

Lay tissue under bodice pattern back and front. Redraw underarm and side seams, adding about ⅜" to each. Taper both lines to nothing above sleeve notches and at waistline.

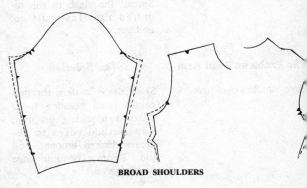

BROAD SHOULDERS

62

The Problem: Short Arm

leeve hangs below desired
ength. Fabric wrinkles and
unches.

The Solution

Lay a fold across sleeve
pattern from side to side at
a slight diagonal. Pin. If
additional length needs to be
taken up, lay another fold
across sleeve pattern near
underarm from side to side
at a slight diagonal in the
opposite direction. Pin.

The Problem: Long Arm

leeve fullness is slightly
bove elbow, above desired
rist length.

The Solution

Slash sleeve pattern from
side to side along diagonal
lines as illustrated. Spread
slashes to desired length. Insert tissue under both slashes, and pin.

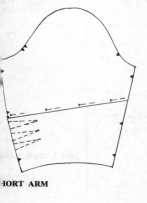

IORT ARM

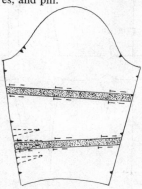

LONG ARM

63

The Problem:
Too-Large Waistline

The Solution

Waistline rides up over natural waistline, causing wrinkling.

Slip tissue under side seam areas of bodice and skirt patterns. Redraw side seams to required width, tapering to underarm and hip. Pin. If additional width is required, each dart around waistline may be let out slightly. Redraw darts, tapering to dart points.

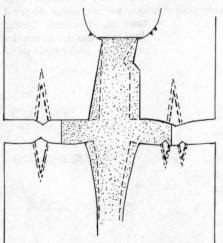

TOO LARGE WAIS

64

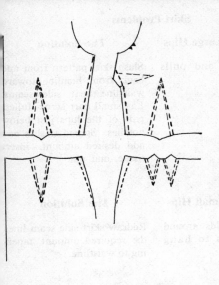

TOO SMALL WAIST

The Problem:
Too-Small Waistline

Waist sags below natural waistline, bodice is too large at waistline.

The Solution

Redraw side seam lines of bodice and skirt patterns, tapering lines to underarm and hip. If additional decrease is needed, each dart around waistline may be redrawn slightly wider. Redraw dart lines, tapering to slightly deeper dart points.

Skirt Problems

The Problem: Large Hips

Skirt rides up and pulls across hipline.

The Solution

Slash skirt pattern front and back from hemline toward waistline near side seams. Lay small dart across fullest part of the hips just below notches. Spread slashes and add desired amount. Insert tissue, and pin.

The Problem: Small Hips

Skirt falls in folds around hips and tends to hang loosely.

The Solution

Redraw skirt side seam lines the required amount, tapering to waistline.

The Problem: Large Rear

Skirt wrinkles across rear and tends to ride up in the back.

The Solution

Slash skirt back pattern through center of dart closest to center back and toward hemline. Slash from center back toward side seam about 7" below waistline. Spread both slashes, keeping center back seam straight. Insert tissue, and pin. Redraw waistline dart that was slashed.

66

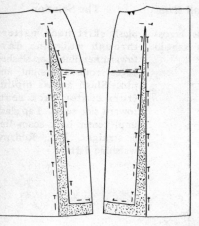

TOO LARGE HIPS

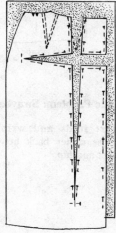

LARGE REAR

The Problem: Small Rear

Skirt falls in folds across rear and tends to sag in back.

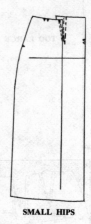

SMALL HIPS

The Solution

Slash skirt back pattern through waistline dart toward hemline. Lap slashed edges required amount, and pin. Slash across hipline from center back seam toward side seam. Lap slash until center back seam line is straight. Pin. Redraw waistline dart.

The Problem: Swayback

Skirt folds and wrinkles across center back between waist and hip.

The Solution

Slash skirt back pattern from center back toward side about 2″ below waistline. Lap slashed edges the desired amount, and pin. Straighten and redraw back waistline dart. Straighten and redraw center back.

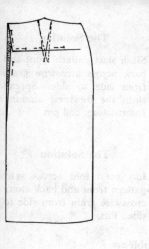

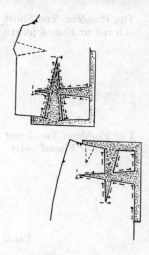

SWAY BACK

LARGE TUMMY

The Problem: Large Tummy

Fabric pulls across skirt front, causing front waistline to ride up over waist.

The Solution

Slash skirt front pattern from center front across toward side about 3″ to 4″ below waistline. Slash waistline dart nearest to center front. Spread both slashes the desired amount. Insert tissue, and pin. Redraw waistline dart to bring waistline back to normal position.

The Problem: Too-Short Gored or Flared Skirt

The Solution

Slash skirt pattern front and back across crosswise grain from side to side. Spread slash the desired amount. Insert tissue, and pin.

The Problem: Too-Long Gored or Flared Skirt

The Solution

Lay even fold across skirt pattern front and back along crosswise grain from side to side. Pin.

Pants Problems

The Problem: Too-Short Crotch

Crotch is uncomfortable, too tight.

The Solution

Slash pants pattern front and back across hip below waistline darts. Spread slash the desired amount. Insert tissue, and pin.

The Problem: Too-Long Crotch

Crotch hangs below desired length, making pants look baggy.

The Solution

Lay an even fold across pants pattern front and back across hip below waistline darts. Pin.

LENGTHWISE GRAIN OF FABRIC

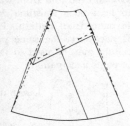

LENGTHWISE GRAIN OF FABRIC

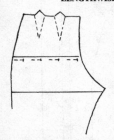
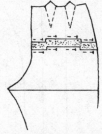

TOO LONG CROTCH   **TOO SHORT CROTCH**

The Problem: Large Hips

Pants look "clingy," follow the body line too closely.

The Solution

Slash pants front pattern near waistline dart from waist to hem. Spread slash required amount, allowing a 2" ease. Insert tissue, and pin.

The Problem: Small Hips

Pants fold around hips, hang loosely.

The Solution

Lay an even fold from waist to hem near waistline dart in pants front pattern. Pin. If necessary, the same procedure may be used to take in pants back pattern.

SMALL HIPS  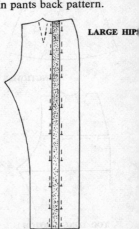 LARGE HIPS

The Problem: Large Waistline	The Solution
	See suggested skirt waistline alterations.

The Problem: Small Waistline	The Solution
	See suggested skirt waistline alterations.

The Problem: Swayback	The Solution
	See suggested skirt swayback alterations.

The Problem: Large Tummy	The Solution
	See suggested skirt tummy alterations.

The Problem: Large Rear	The Solution
Pants pull across rear and tend to wrinkle just below rear.	Slash pants back pattern pattern. Redraw side seam from waistline, tapering to point just below fullest part of hip. Redraw waistline darts to widen and deepen them. An additional alteration may be made by redrawing leg seam at crotch and tapering back to seam at thigh.

73

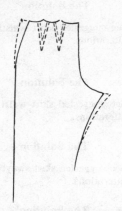
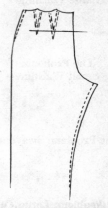

The Problem: Flat Rear

Pants bag across rear.

The Solution

Slash pants back pattern from back seam toward side seam below waistline dart points. Lap slashed edges the required amount, and pin. Redraw side seam line and center back seam line.

Check and Double-check—with a Pin Fitting

Every pattern piece of your new fashion that needed alteration has been altered. And now comes a final check —a pin fitting—to make sure every line and detail is just where it should be.

Start your pin-fitting from the inside out, with the undergarments and shoes you intend to wear when your fashion is finished.

Then, pin together the bodice front and back pattern pieces and slip them on. If all your alterations are satisfactory, the bodice should fit perfectly—or at least as well as a tissue pattern can fit.

Next, pin in and check the sleeve pattern for fit and, finally, pin together the skirt pattern pieces, pinning in all darts, of course.

Check the skirt for easy, comfortable fit. Pin skirt and bodice together and let yourself imagine how lovely the finished fashion will be.

If, in spite of your careful alterations and fine fit, the pattern somehow seems not as flattering as you'd hoped, a few more minor adjustments may help. But if you've selected a fashion that is out-and-out unflattering, stop now. You may be disappointed—and you've surely lost the price of your nonreturnable pattern—but how much greater your disappointment would be if you had spent time cutting and basting and sewing an unflattering fashion.

If, however, your pin-fitting is successful—if fit and fashion have come together as well as you hoped they would—you're ready to prepare your fabric for cutting.

CHAPTER 4

The Fabric
of Fashion

A fabric counter, to a sewer, can be as exciting a place as a candy counter is to a child.

Each offers a dazzling display of confections, and a final selection is not easy for a child—or a sewer. But the wrong choice can give a child an ache in the tummy—or a sewer an ache in the head.

Not too many years ago, a fabric buyer could make her selection almost entirely on touch. A piece of wool was just that—warm, springy to the touch, resilient, able to return to its original shape even after being crushed. Silk was lustrous, elegant, difficult to crease. Linen was smooth, cool, heavier than cotton. And cotton was just cotton—practical, long-wearing, and not very elegant.

But that was before scientists in their laboratories turned their hand to the development of synthetic fabrics.

Today, fabric counters are filled with yards and yards of fabrics that never came off the back of a sheep or from the cocoon of a silkworm or never were grown in the fields.

Today, the choice of fabrics, textures, patterns, designs, and colors available to the home sewer is almost beyond imagination.

Weaving—the Ancient Art

The basic art of weaving hasn't changed much through the years, although some of the yarns being woven into fabric today weren't even imagined just a few short years ago.

Fiber—natural or man-made—is made into strands that are twisted into yarns that are woven into cloth.

To weave the cloth, lengthwise yarns—they're called the warp—are interlaced with a set of crosswise yarns—called the woof, weft, or filler. These lengthwise and crosswise yarns are known to sewers as the "grain line" or the "straight of the goods." They are vitally important to proper fit and the proper hang of a garment as you'll see in chapter 6.

So, whenever you shop for fabric, always examine it carefully to make sure the grain lines run true—that is, the lengthwise threads run exactly parallel to the selvage edge and crosswise threads run exactly perpendicular to lengthwise threads.

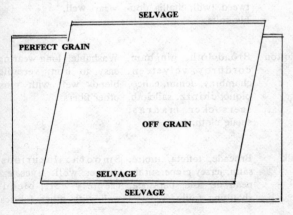

SELVAGE

PERFECT GRAIN

OFF GRAIN

SELVAGE

SELVAGE

77

Fabrics: Getting to Know Them

Fabrics have their own special personalities, very muc[h]
as people do. Some are soft and clingy; others are cris[p]
and to-the-point. The more you know about fabrics—ho[w]
to show them off to best advantage and how to have the[m]
show you off to best advantage—the better you'll be ab[le]
to achieve that perfect marriage of pattern and fabric.

For a quick review of what fabric can do for you, se[e]
chapter 1. And for details of some of today's marvelou[s]
fabrics and their special personalities, see the followin[g]
chart.

Fiber	Type of Fabric	Characteristics
Wool	Gabardine, jersey, broadcloth, flannel, tweed, twill, challis, double knits	Warm, absorbent, wrin[k]kle-resistant; dyes wel[l] wears well.
Cotton	Broadcloth, gingham, corduroy, velveteen, chambray, denim, calico, piquè, chintz, sailcloth, seersucker, madras, suede cloth, lace	Washable, long-wearin[g] easy to iron; versatil[e] blends well with mos[t] other fibers.
Silk	Brocade, taffeta, moiré, satin, jersey crepe, surah, peau de soie, barathea, shantung, faille	Smooth, luxurious drapes well; dyes ex[-] tremely well; blend[s] well with other fabric[s]

78

Linen	Suiting, crash, damask, dress linen, handkerchief linen	Crisp, cool, comfortable, absorbent; shrinks unless treated; wrinkles unless treated.
Rayon	Crepe, shantung, velvet, flannel, satin, linen-weave, faille	Drapes and dyes well; can be textured and finished in a wide variety of ways; blends well with other fibers.
Acetate	Taffeta, bengaline, jersey, satin, surah, faille, crepe	Soft, luxurious; easy to drape; dyes extremely well; moth- and mildew-resistant; tendency to fade; can be permanently pleated.
Acrylic	Suiting, flannel, jersey, crepe, fake fur, double knit	Luxurious feel; warmth and bulk without weight; does not stretch, sag, or wrinkle; resistant to damage from mildew, moths, sunlight.
Nylon	Crepe, knits, jersey, ottoman, plissé	Tough, elastic, strong; drapes well; sometimes difficult to dye; resists wrinkles; pleats well; resistant to damage from mildew, moths; sometimes sensitive to strong sun; has a tendency to pull.

Polyester	Broadcloth, crepe, poplin, jersey, knits, double knits, sailcloth	Strong, wrinkle-resistant; drapes well; pleats well when pleats are baked in; resistant to damage from mildew, moths, sunlight; sometimes sensitive to heat.

Note: This chart covers some of the major fibers and fabrics in common use today. There are others, of course, and the list is growing as new synthetics are developed. To keep abreast of the latest fabrics, skim through the fashion magazines—or browse through the fabric counters, keeping an eye on the hang tags listing fiber content.

Usual Widths Available	Tips for Use	Tips for Care and Sewing
54", 60"	Suits, coats, tailored dresses, sportswear	Dry-clean unless labeled otherwise; iron with press cloth and moderate iron; sponge before sewing unless fabric has been preshrunk. *See* SPECIAL TIPS FOR SEWING JERSEY AND DOUBLE KNITS *(page 86).*

80

35", 36", 45"	Sportswear, tailored dresses, suits (heavy weight cottons), evening wear (lace, velveteen)	Use hot iron and press while damp; cotton blends may be wash-and-wear, so check hang tag for specific laundering instructions. *See* SPECIAL TIPS FOR SEWING VELVET, VELVETEEN, CORDUROY *(page 91);* LACE *(page 87);* WASH-AND-WEAR *(page 92).*
39", 42"	Soft, draped dresses, cocktail dresses, dressmaker coats and suits, evening wear	Dry-clean unless labeled otherwise; iron with press cloth and moderate iron. *See* SPECIAL TIPS FOR SEWING SILK *(page 89).*
35", 36"	Tailored dresses, tailored and dressmaker suits, sportswear	Use hot iron and press while damp; raw seam edges will ravel without special finishing; cut, don't tear, along crosswise thread to straighten.
39," 45",	Tailored dresses, cocktail dresses, evening wear	Press with warm iron; check hang tag for cleaning or washing instructions.
39", 45" 50"	Sportswear, soft draped dresses, cocktail dresses, evening wear	Dry-clean or handwash; press with cool iron while damp; keep away from heat and nail polish removers.

Usual Widths Available	Tips for Use	Tips for Care and Sewing
45", 48" for jersey and crepe 54", 60" for flannels, suiting, fake furs	Sportswear, tailored dresses, suits, coats, ponchos	All acrylics should be washed before cutting; check hang tag carefully for ironing instructions. *See* SPECIAL TIPS FOR SEWING KNITS *(page 86);* FAKE FURS *(page 85);* BONDED FABRICS *(page 84).*
45"	Sportswear, tailored dresses, suits	Most nylons are wash-and-wear, but check hang tag to be sure; iron gently with warm iron. *See* SPECIAL TIPS FOR SEWING WASH-AND-WEAR FABRIC: *(page 92).*
45", 54"; 54", 60" for knits	Sportswear, tailored dresses	Washable, quick-drying; iron with warm iron if necessary. *See* SPECIAL TIPS FOR SEWING KNITS *(page 86).*

From Fiber to Fabric to Finish

The miracle of modern chemistry doesn't stop with the creation of new fibers and fabrics. It has also reached out to provide exciting new finishes for old and new fabrics alike.

Drip-dry, crease-resistant, mothproof, mildew-proof, color-fast: these are some of the processes the men in the laboratories have developed to make fabric selection more fun—and just a little confusing.

Be sure to double-check the hang tags or labels on the bolts of fabric to learn exactly what finish has—or has not—been applied and what you can expect from the fabric as a result.

DRIP-DRY FINISHES usually make fabric easier to machine-wash, more resistant to wrinkling, easier to iron, or make ironing unnecessary.

CREASE-RESISTANT FINISHES usually make fabric more resistant to creasing and wrinkling.

SHRINKAGE-CONTROL FINISHES usually reduce the amount fabric will shrink during washing or dry cleaning.

WATER-REPELLANT FINISHES usually make fabric resistant to water-spotting.

MOTHPROOFING FINISHES usually protect fabric from moth damage.

COLOR-FAST PROCESSES usually make fabric resistant to color running when laundered.

INSULATING PROCESSES usually give fabric additional warmth during winter, additional coolness during summer.

Who knows what new processes and finishes will be developed to solve other fabric problems? You will—if you keep your eye on the latest fashion magazines.

The New Fabrics—They're Fabulous!

Fake furs, stretch fabrics, bonded fabrics, look-like-leathers, cotton suedes, velvety no-wale corduroys: they're new, exciting, and like no other fabric you've worked with before. They can perk up a routine wardrobe; they can add interest and variety to your fashions—and they can be a problem if you don't know how to handle them.

But don't back away from these fabulous fabrics just because they need a bit of special handling.

The following section will offer some helpful hints for handling these marvelous modern fabrics—and some of your old favorites, too.

Bonded Fabrics

Bonded fabrics are actually two fabrics in one—the fashion fabric and a tricot fabric that has been bonded to the underside. This tricot bonding usually eliminates the need for lining or underlining.

Pattern selection: Avoid fashions with circular skirts or draped lines. Tailored patterns with top-stitched detail would be an excellent selection.

Cutting and marking: Always fold fabric wrong side together and lay pattern on right side. Use lots of pins with fine, sharp points. Mark with tailor tacks or chalk pencil.

Stitching: Use mercerized or synthetic thread. Machine stitch, using 12 to 15 stitches per inch. Do *not* pull fabric as it passes under machine foot since this may cause puckering.

Seams: No special seam finish is required because fabric will not ravel. However, slash darts to eliminate bulk.

Hems: Hem edge can be pinked and sewn with a French stitch. Be careful to catch the hem to the tricot backing only.

Chiffon

Chiffon is a sheer, filmy fabric that has a tendency to shift as you cut it because of its filminess.

Pattern selection: Avoid fashions with intricate cuts and many pattern pieces. Full-skirted fashions would be excellent selections.

Cutting and marking: Fold fabric lengthwise, matching selvages and ends. Pin or baste these together to prevent shifting. Don't try to cut chiffon on a slick cutting surface. Lay an old sheet or tablecloth over the surface and lay chiffon on this. Try to lay out and pin the entire pattern before cutting. Use more pins than usual to pin pattern to fabric and cut with sharp scissors. Don't lift fabric as you cut. You can eliminate unsightly show-through facings by cutting the bodice section double or by cutting bodice front facing in one piece with bodice.

Stitching: Use mercerized cotton or silk thread. Machine-stitch, using 15 to 18 stitches per inch. Make sure your needle is *very* sharp. To prevent any catching while sewing, it is a good idea to stitch over tissue paper and tear it away after stitching.

Seams: To maintain the illusion of filminess, French seams and hand-rolled edges are strongly recommended *(see chapter 8).*

Fake Furs

These fabulous fakes often look as if they've come right off the back of some wild animal—or off no animal ever seen in the jungle.

Pattern selection: Avoid fashions with intricate detailing, especially for high-napped fabrics. Simple sportswear vests, jackets, coats, slacks, and ponchos would be excellent selections.

Cutting and marking: Most fake furs can be cut with the nap running down, following pattern instructions for cutting napped fabrics. However, if the fur pattern is highly distinctive, it may be necessary to cut each piece separately for perfect matching.

Stitching: Many fake furs have a tendency to slip as they are machine-stitched, so seams should be basted first. Machine-stitch, using 8 to 10 stitches per inch. Check carefully to make sure pile is not caught in seams. A sharp-pointed needle will help to pull pile out of seam. Slash and open darts and eliminate seam bulk wherever possible.

Pressing: Never press with a steam iron. It will cause the fabric to mat. Use the tip of a dry iron and a dry press cloth to open seams.

Closings: Try to avoid making buttonholes wherever possible. Loop closings, frogs, and hooks are recommended instead.

Jersey and Double Knits

The suppleness of jersey and double knits makes them extremely popular for many of today's fashions—and those made of synthetic fibers are virtually care-free.

Pattern selection: There is almost no limit to the fashionable face of jersey and double knits. Dresses, both tailored and draped, sportswear, coats and suits, even evening wear can be beautifully fashioned from them. Do, however, be careful to choose the proper weight for the fashion you have in mind, and avoid bias-cut skirts because of the possibility of excess stitching.

Cutting and marking: Single knits like jerseys most often come in tubular form—with two fold lines instead of one. But these fold lines are usually stretched off line so you'll need to refold or slit the fabric along a lengthwise rib near the fold line to establish the true lengthwise grain of the fabric. Most double knits come folded like woolens, with right or face side inside, and can be handled with the same ease as woolens. Some single knits have a tendency to curl when they are cut, so extra pins along cutting lines are helpful.

Stitching: Always stay-stitch immediately after cutting to prevent the pattern piece from stretching out of shape. Machine-stitch with polyester thread, using 12 to 15 stitches per inch. If top-stitching is required, lengthen stitch to 8 to 10 per inch.

Seams: Shoulder, neckline, and waistline seams should be stabilized with straight seam binding. Do this by cutting strips of straight seam binding to proper size, pinning each *under* the seam to be stitched and including binding *in the seam* as you machine-stitch. Since most knits do not ravel, special seam finishes are unnecessary. However, to prevent seam edges from curling, stitch about ¼″ from cut edge.

Lining: Most single knits like jerseys should be skirt-lined with a soft, lightweight lining. Most double knits rarely require lining and, as a matter of fact, lose some of their suppleness when they are lined.

Hems: Always allow knit fashions to hang at least twenty-four hours before hemming. This will help to ensure a straight hem.

Lace

The filmy, cobwebby look of lace, as an accent or as an overall fabric, has always been an important part of the fashion picture. Today's laces can be made by hand or by machine, of silk, rayon, cotton, nylon, or a combination of several yarns.

Pattern selection: Since lace has its own lovely pattern, it is advisable to select a simple fashion without intricate detailing. Dresses, coats, evening wear, even pants suits can be fashioned from lace—but be careful to select the proper weight of lace for the fashion you're planning to make.

Cutting and marking: Some laces have an up-and-down pattern and must be cut with all pattern pieces laid in the same direction. Always try to keep the lace pattern intact. Fold lace with wrong sides together and use extremely sharp pins to pin pattern pieces to fabric. To avoid snagging, always place pins within seam allowances and cut with sharp scissors. Use tailor tacks for marking.

Stitching: Always hand-baste seams together before machine-stitching to prevent slipping. Machine-stitch with silk thread for silk, wool, or synthetic lace, mercerized thread for cotton and linen lace. Machine-stitch, using 15 stitches per inch, and be careful not to pull or stretch lace as it moves through the foot. In some cases, especially where a scalloped edging is to be used, it is best to hand- or machine-appliqué the seams together.

Seams: If seams will be hidden because of an opaque underlining, they may be pinked and pressed open. If you are using a sheer underlining, consider French seams and hand-rolled edges to maintain the illusion of filminess.

Laminated Fabrics

Laminated fabrics are another two-for-one fashion development for the home sewer. A backing of synthetic foam is laminated or heat-set to adhere permanently to a face fabric, thereby eliminating the need for interfacing, although a lining helps to protect the foam backing.

Pattern selection: Laminated fabrics are especially suitable for coats, jackets, sportswear, and children's wear provided you choose patterns with easy fit and a minimum of darts and seam details.

Cutting and marking: Always place pattern on the right side of the fabric so you can accurately follow the grain lines. If the foam backing has a tendency to stick together when folded, it would be wise to cut a single layer of fabric at a time. Cut with a large, sharp scissors. Mark with tailor tacks, chalk, or pins.

Stitching: Always hand-baste to prevent fabric from slipping and as an accurate double-check for fit. Stay-stitch all bias and curved seams. To prevent foam from sticking as it feeds through the foot, slip a strip of tissue below seam and a strip of bias above seam. Sew bias right into the seam but tear away tissue. Machine-stitch with mercerized or synthetic thread, using 10 stitches per inch.

Seams: Grade all seam allowances carefully to eliminate as much bulk as possible. Faced edges should be topstitched to keep them flat. Top-stitch seams for a neat, tailored finish as well as extra strength. Finger-press seams open wherever possible. If pressing is necessary, use a steam iron at medium setting, but *do not* let iron touch the foam.

Silk

Silk—the elegant one—remains the favorite of many fashionable women because of its luster, its brilliant colors, its marvelous hand, and its ability to "go anywhere in style."

Pattern selection: The weight of the silk you choose is almost the only guide you need for selecting a pattern. Soft, lightweight silks make marvelous dresses and blouses; sheer silks grace cocktail dresses and evening wear; heavy silks make elegant suits and coats.

Cutting and marking: Silk may slip and slide on your normal cutting surface, so follow general instructions for cutting chiffon *(see page 85).*

Stitching: Hand-baste seams and darts rather than machine-baste because many silks will show every needle mark. Machine-stitch with silk thread, using 15 to 20 stitches per inch for sheer and soft silks, 12 stitches per inch for heavier silks.

Seams: Finish seams to guarantee as little bulk as possible.

Lining: For elegance as much as for shape retention, most silk fashions should be lined or underlined.

Stretch Fabrics

People stretch—and now, so do stretch fabrics, thanks to the weaving in of stretch threads to any number of classic fabrics like denim, terrycloth, gabardine, and corduroy. But the fabric you select should be carefully examined to see which way the stretch goes—lengthwise, crosswise, or both—and how it will work in the pattern of your choice.

Pattern selection: Active sportswear is ideally suited to the stretch fabrics. Make your pattern selection in your usual size, but double-check your final fit. You mav *not* need the full ease allowance.

Cutting and marking: Lay out the pattern pieces in the direction of the stretch desired. Be careful not to pull or stretch fabric as you cut. In fact, *never* let part of fabric hang over the edge of your cutting table as you cut.

Stitching: Nonstretch seams—those not cut in the direction of the stretch—may be handled like any regular seam. Stretch seams, however, must be sewed so the thread stretches *with* the seam. Use a small zigzag stitch with a zigzag sewing machine. With a regular sewing machine, use stretch thread and stretch seam as you sew. The seam will snap back to its original length after it is sewn.

Seams: If your stretch fabric ravels, you must use a secure seam finish.

Pressing: Never push iron along seams. Use an up-and-down ironing motion instead. Seams that have rippled slightly during sewing should recover completely when they are lightly steamed.

Velvet, Velveteen, and Corduroy

Velvet, velveteen, and corduroy are napped-surface fabrics with the kind of versatility that makes them a home sewer's favorite for herself, her family, even her home.

Pattern selection: Many sportswear, daytime, and evening and formal patterns are suitable for these elegant napped fabrics, but those that turn out most successfully feature simple lines without fussy details.

Cutting and marking: Make sure to check and follow the pattern layout for napped fabrics. All pieces *must* be laid in one direction; nap running toward the hem for longer wear; nap running toward the face to emphasize a particularly rich color. It is helpful to cut off all pattern margins before laying out pieces. Fabric should be cut pile side up or wrong sides together. Use extremely sharp pins and pin wherever possible along seam allowances to avoid marring or matting down the pile. Make tailor tacks with silk thread.

Stitching: Always baste with silk thread and double-check fit before machine-stitching. Machine-stitch velvet with silk thread, velveteen and corduroy with silk or mercerized thread. Machine-stitch, using 10 to 12 stitches per inch. Do *not* top-stitch. Wherever possible, try to stitch *with* the pile.

Seams: Seams may be bound, overcast, or pinked to give a finished edge. To eliminate bulk in areas where facings are necessary, use a firm, lighter-weight facing fabric like taffeta.

Pressing: Velvet, velveteen, and corduroy must be pressed with great care because of their pile. *See chapter 7 for complete pressing instructions.*

Wash-and-Wear Fabrics

Today's wash-and-wear fabrics are a boon to a busy woman, but the very characteristics that make them resist wrinkling may make them a bit difficult to sew.

Pattern selection: Avoid elaborate seam details in the pattern of your choice; otherwise almost anything goes.

Cutting and marking: Double-check to make sure your fabric is straight of grain—that the crosswise threads are at exact right angles with the lengthwise threads or the selvage edge. If the fabric is *not* straight of grain, it will need to be squared *(see page 122)*. If possible, press out the center crease before laying out pattern pieces. If crease cannot be pressed out, try to pin around it so it will not appear in the finished fashion. Pin with sharp pins and cut with a sharp scissors. Do *not* mark with a wax chalk because the marks may not be removable.

Stitching: Use mercerized or synthetic thread, depending on the fiber content of the fabric. Test-stitch on a swatch of fabric to make sure the seams don't pucker. Adjust your tensions and stitch length accordingly, although a 12-to-an-inch stitch should work on most wash-and-wear fabrics. Always stitch slowly and check for puckering. If the seam is smooth after stitching and before ironing, it will stay that way washing after washing.

Interfacings: Always select wash-and-wear interfacing fabric.

What Shapes the Fabric of Fashion?

First, *you* do—with the darts, seams, shirrs, gathers, drapes, pleats, and folds that are an integral part of the fashion you're constructing.

But three important kinds of additional shaping stand by to underscore the lines of your fashion. They are UN-DERLINING, INTERFACING, and LINING.

They work this way:

Underlining is cut from the same pattern pieces as the outer fashion. It serves as a kind of second skin for your fashion, adding crispness and contour and body and helping to control stretching and wrinkling.

Not every fashion needs underlining—in fact, some of the modern fabrics have excellent body, which lasts well through repeated launderings or dry cleanings. And some fashions, especially those that feature delicate draping, may need different kinds of underlining—lightweight to underscore the draping, for example, and firmer weight to underscore the skirt.

Interfacing is used to support and reinforce specific finishing details like facings, collars, cuffs, pockets, and buttonholes. It is available in woven and nonwoven fabrics,

in sew-on and press-on types, and in weights to suit ever
need.

Lining is a protective covering that hides constructio
details, helps to preserve the outer shape, prevents stretch
ing and wrinkling, and adds a custom look to your fashion

Some outer garments—winter coats and jackets—nee
an extra lining to provide additional warmth. This extra
lining, or interlining, is usually placed between the linin
and the underlining.

Fusing Fabrics—Lining of the Future

It just may be that the men in the laboratories have
found a way to make most underlinings obsolete. They ca
their new product a *polymerized fiber web,* and it can be
fused to the inside of a fabric with the heat and pressure o
your steam iron.

The web looks very much like a piece of transfer paper
roughly textured on one side, and can be purchased by the
yard to use as you need it.

If this fiber web is available at the yard goods counte
where you shop, why not try a few experiments with it
Read the instruction sheet carefully and see if it can help
you sew more quickly and easily.

The Shapers—How to Select the Right Ones

You've spent much time and effort selecting the right
fabric for your new fashion. Now, shouldn't you spend
almost as much time and effort selecting the shaping mate
rial that will underscore that fabric perfectly?

Of course you should.

Here are the key questions you'll need to answer as you
select the right shaping material:

94

- Is the shaping fabric the right weight for the fashion fabric?

- Will it give the desired amount of stiffness? The desired amount of flexibility?

- Is the texture and finish of the shaping material similar to the texture and finish of the fashion fabric?

- Is a combination of several kinds and weights of shaping fabric necessary to give the proper support in different areas?

- Is the color of the shaping fabric suitable for use under the fashion fabric?

- Will the shaping fabric react to laundering and dry cleaning the same way the fashion fabric does?

Summing Up: The Shapers

Only you can judge the precise effect you want in your new fashion. Are you after the merest hint of body? Do you want crisp shaping? Does your fabric call for firm support—or very gentle support?

Before you make your final selection, try draping both fashion fabric and shaping fabric together over your hand. Make sure they work well together—that the shaping fabric enhances the fashion fabric and, together, they'll enhance the lines of your pattern.

The following chart highlights *some* of the many shaping fabrics available—and some of their broadly suggested uses:

Fashion Fabric	Lining and Underlining	Interfacing
Heavyweight coatings and suitings	Taffeta, muslin, Milium®, organza, acetate, China silk, SiBonne®, Under-Current®, brocade	Heavy hair canvas, Pellon®, Interlon® Shape-flex®
Mediumweight Woolens and synthetics	China silk, acetate, SiBonne®, Under-Current®, Super-Siri®, organza, taffeta, About Face®	Hair canvas, Pellon®, Interlon® Shape-Flex®
Lightweight Wools	China silk, organza, SiBonne®, acetate, voile, UnderCurrent®	Light hair canvas, Pellon®, Interlon® Shape-Flex®
Lace, Chiffon, Sheer Wools	Taffeta, peau de soie, silk organza, net, marquisette, chiffon	Organza, organdy, marquisette
Dry-Cleanable Cottons and Linens	Preshrunk batiste or voile, China silk, SiBonne®, Under-Current®	Lightweight Pellon® lightweight Interlon®, lightweight Sta-Shape®
Lightweight Wash-and-Wear	Cotton organza, preshrunk batiste, About Face®, Keynote Plus®	Armo Press®, Sta-Shape® durable press, Pellon®, Interlon® durable press

And Finally—the Fashionable Notions

Your fashion fabric has been carefully selected. Your shaping fabric has been just as carefully selected. And now you need those fashionable notions—they're listed on the back of your pattern envelope—that add the final touch to your new fashion.

Many of the standard notions you keep on hand with the rest of your sewing supplies. *(See chapter 5, page 118, for a check-list of standard notions.)*

But you may need any or all of the following specialized notions for your new fashion—and the best time to buy them is at the same time you buy both pattern and fabric.

You may need:

Belting—standard widths range from ½" to 3"; available in black or white; by the yard or prepackaged in regular or iron-on types.

Bias tape—made of cotton in ¼", ½", and 1" widths; available in a range of colors in single- or double-fold.

Boning—is usually made of nylon and covered with white or black fabric; used wherever stiffness is needed to mold or maintain shape; available by the yard or in prepackaged strips.

Braid trims—available in a wide variety of colors and styles.

Buckles—are available in a wide variety of shapes and sizes, in silver, gold, or colors, or ready to be custom-covered; they may be purchased separately or as part of a prepackaged belting kit.

Buttons—the well-chosen buttons should enhance your fashion rather than merely finish it. Buttons are available in two general types, sew-through and shank; in a wide variety of sizes, shapes, colors, and finishes. Button kits for covering and customizing are also available.

Cording—standard diameters range from ⅛" to 1"; of cotton, cellulose, or synthetic fibers. Cording is used as a filler for piping, tubing, buttonholes; heavier weights may be used for drawstrings or belting filler.

Elastic—standard widths range from ¼″ to 1¼″; in white, pink, or black; sold by the yard or in prepackaged lengths. Also available drawstring elastic, a round, cordlike elastic for making castings; and elastic thread for shirred accents.

Eyelets—for belts, lacing, and fashion accents are available in kits.

Grosgrain ribbon—standard widths range from ³⁄₁₆″ to 3⅛″ or even wider; available in a wide range of colors; sold by the yard; ideal for staying waistlines and for a variety of decorative uses.

Gripper snaps—available individually or preattached to tape sold by the yard; a gripper kit is necessary to fasten individual grippers; ideal for hard usage on sportswear, pajamas, children's clothes, work clothes.

Hem facing—bias stripping 2½″ wide with folded edges, available prepackaged in cotton or rayon taffeta.

Horsehair braid—standard widths range from ½″ to 6″; in black or white; used to give hem support to lightweight full skirts and lace fashions.

Lace Seam Binding—an elegant seam and hem finish available in widths of ½″ or ¾″; cotton or elasticized in a range of colors; always preshrink to avoid puckering. *(See page 126)*

Lingerie Strapholders—another elegant "inside" touch, to keep lingerie straps from wandering; available in black, white, and pink.

Nylon closure tape—available in standard 1″ width by the yard; it consists of two strips that intermesh when pressed together; useful for attaching removable

ollars and cuffs, closing slipcovers, belts, jackets, and
waistbands.

Piping—a corded bias strip ⅛″ wide with a ¼″ seam
allowance for use as a decorative edge trimming; available prepackaged or by the yard in cotton in a wide range
of colors.

Seam binding—the indispensable sewing notion in wash-
and-wear, iron-on, rayon, and bias versions; available in
prepackaged lengths in ½″ and 1″ widths in a variety of
colors.

Shoulder pads—in a variety of shapes to correct figure
faults, provided a necessary shoulder foundation, or emphasize a particular shoulder line; available covered or
uncovered.

Stays—available in 4″, 6″, and 8″ lengths; of metal
plastic, or bone; used to shape, mold, or reinforce.

Twill tape—standard widths range from ¼″ to 1″ in
black or white only; used for tailoring and staying waistlines.

Weights—available in various sizes and weights; made
of lead and used to weight hems or collars or emphasize
particular fashion effects; also available by the yard as
tiny lead pellets encased in fabric.

Zippers—the popular closing made of metal or nylon
in a variety of styles, weights, lengths, and colors to fill
almost every closing need. The most common are; neckline, dress placket, skirt placket, trousers, separating.

CHAPTER **5**

Sewing "Tools of
the Trade"

Every craftsman needs them; those special tools that make it possible to do the job most efficiently.

The artist needs the right brushes, paints, palette knives, canvas tools. The cook needs the right pots, pans, measuring tools. And the sewer needs the right pins, needles, threads, scissors, markers, sewing machine—and a neatly organized sewing area.

Sewing Space—How To Get It

The dream of every creative sewer is to have her very own sewing room, complete with large cutting table, permanently mounted sewing machine, lots of drawer space for pattern, notion, and fabric storage, and lots of hanging space for half-finished fashions. This sewing "dream room" would have an ironing board and all the tools of ironing within easy reach and would, of course, look like something out of the pages of an elegant home furnishings magazine.

If you are one of the fortunate few who have the physical

space and the financial wherewithal to manage such a sewing room, stop dreaming and get on with your planning.

Plan plentiful and well-directed lighting, carefully organized storage areas for everything from scissors and threads to large, flat cuts of fabrics, and enough counter space to take you from initial cutting to final pressing with room to spare.

Getting Around the Space Problem

So you don't have a twelve-foot by fifteen-foot room for your exclusive sewing use. But do you have a little corner

somewhere that can be converted into a sewing nook? Or a closet that be turned into a compact sewing area?

A SEWING NOOK can be made from a bare wall or an unused corner with a bit of effort and a lot of clever planning. Place a small table against the bare wall and hang a large pegboard above it. In the order that best suits your needs, hang spools of thread, scissors, and sewing notions.

A small unpainted chest, decorated to your taste, makes an ideal storage area and adds work counter space if it is placed next to your table. A straight-back chair, a hanging full-length mirror, and good lighting will complete your handy little sewing nook.

A CLOSET with clothes bar removed can also be turned into a convenient sewing area with a bit of imagination. At table height along the back wall of the closet, hang a hinged board just wide enough to clear the closet sides and long enough to skim the closet floor. An unpainted chest mounted on wheels can be rolled out of the closet to serve as a support base for the hinged board, and as an additional storage area. Inside the closet, shelves and pegboard provide additional storage. A straight-back chair, a table lamp, and a full-length mirror hung on the closet door complete the transformation of your closet into a sewing area.

"I Can't Spare a Closet!"

Even if space is at an absolute premium in your home, you can still find room for a sewing storage center—under your bed!

Large underbed storage boxes are commercially available. With a bit of clever partitioning—small sections for notions, larger sections for pattern storage, and even larger sections for fabric storage—you'll be able to keep your sewing needs well organized while taking up the least bit of space possible.

Making the Best of It with Planning

Dream room, sewing nook, converted closet, or underbed storage—you can make the best of what you have by considering the following "necessaries" for ideal sewing conditions. Modify and adapt where you must, but the closer you come to these optimum conditions, the more you'll enjoy your ventures into sewing.

- GOOD LIGHTING, both natural and artificial.

- HANDY OUTLETS for all your electrical equipment, and extension cords where necessary.

- A LARGE, HARD CUTTING SURFACE with easy access on all sides and high enough so you won't need to bend or stoop as you cut.

- FREE MOVEMENT around your sewing machine area and a comfortable, straight-back chair.

- A PRESSING AREA close to your sewing machine.

- A CONVENIENT STORAGE METHOD to keep your sewing needs close at hand and easily accessible as you work.

- CLOSET SPACE to hang partially finished projects.

- A FULL-LENGTH MIRROR—a three-way mirror is ideal—to double-check hang and fit.

- WASTE FACILITIES—even a large paper bag will do—to keep sewing scraps from traveling out of your sewing area.

Your Sewing Machine:
Prime "Tool of the Trade"

The sewing machine, proud offspring of the Industrial Revolution, has become an essential household appliance to millions of women. But any resemblance to the sewing machine of the early days has long since vanished.

Today's home sewing machines are a marvel of modern engineering and have been designed to fit almost everyone's sewing needs and level of skills.

Today's sewing machines are available in three basic types:

- STRAIGHT-STITCH machines, which sew only forward and backward, although attachments are available to permit zigzag stitching.

- ZIGZAG machines, which sew forward and backward and can stitch from side to side.

- AUTOMATIC-STITCH machines, which sew forward, backward, and from side to side and can produce a variety of decorative and other stitches by means of built-in templates or discs.

Each of the above types is also available in cabinet or portable models, and many may be had with slant-needle construction to allow for greater visibility as you sew.

Choosing Your Sewing Machine

Your own particular needs will determine which type of sewing machine is best for you. And some careful comparison shopping will help you decide which machine in the type of your choice is most comfortable and efficient for you to handle.

Make your final choice slowly, carefully, and wisely—and only after test-sewing first—because you and your machine will be working together for a long, long time.

Getting to Know Your Sewing Machine

Just about everything you need to know about your new sewing machine—from operation to maintenance—can be found in the instruction manual that comes with it.

Read it; study it; keep it close at hand whenever you sew.

You'll learn how the basic parts operate: the light switch, stitch selector, take-up lever, and tension adjustment, among others. Most important, you'll learn how to thread your sewing machine properly, how to prepare and insert the bobbin, and how to adjust the thread tension to get a perfect stitch.

Threading the machine: No machine, not even the finest one, will sew properly if it is not threaded properly. Check and double-check your instruction manual until you can thread your machine correctly as automatically as you blink your eyes.

Winding the bobbin: Bobbins wind differently on different machines, but all bobbins should be wound evenly and never so fully that there is friction when the bobbin is placed in the bobbin case.

Adjusting the thread tension: Your instruction manual will undoubtedly show illustrations of the perfect stitch and indicate the necessary adjustments to achieve it. Test-stitch on a bit of scrap fabric to make sure each stitch is perfect. It helps to use a different color for the upper thread and the bobbin thread when you test-stitch. And always test-stitch *before* beginning a new project, since different fabrics may require different tensions.

Stitching Problems—and Causes

Now and then, you may run across any of the following problems:

Breaking of needle:

- Wrong size needle for thread and fabric (*see Needle and Thread Charts on pages 119 to 121*)

- Needle bent

- Needle striking improperly fastened presser foot or attachments

- Trying to sew too thick a seam

Breaking of upper thread:

- Knot in thread

- Improper threading

- Upper tension too tight

- Needle not properly inserted in needle clamp

Breaking of bobbin thread:

- Improper threading of bobbin case

- Knot in bobbin thread

- Bobbin tension too tight

Skipping of stitches:

- Needle not properly inserted in needle clamp

- Needle in backward

- Needle threaded incorrectly

Puckered seams:

- Tension too tight

- Stitch not correct for fabric *(see Needle and Thread Charts on pages 119 to 121)*

- Wrong presser foot

The Time-savers—
Sewing Machine Attachments

Make the most of your sewing machine by learning how to use the attachments that come with it—or that are available for purchase. They'll save you lots of time and help you to get that truly professional look as you sew.

Special feet for your sewing machine include:

A **Zipper foot**—designed so that you can stitch very close to a raised edge, like cording or a zipper.

B **Invisible zipper foot**—designed to stitch an invisible zipper; usually adaptable to both zipper and machine style by means of plastic parts.

C **Hemming foot**—designed to form and stitch a perfect hem without basting or pressing in advance. It is also used to attach ruffles, lace, or any decorative trim.

D **Gathering foot**—designed to lock uniform fullness into each stitch. It is used for shirring and gathering.

E **Roller foot**—designed to feed hard-to-handle fabrics like nylon or vinyl without slipping.

F **Button foot**—designed to hold a 2- or 4-hole button firmly for zigzag or automatic stitching.

G **Binder foot**—designed to apply bias binding to an unfinished edge without pinning or basting in advance.

108

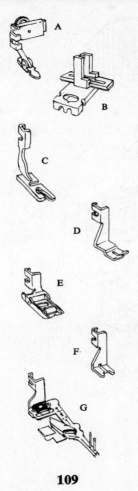

A

B

C

D

E

F

G

109

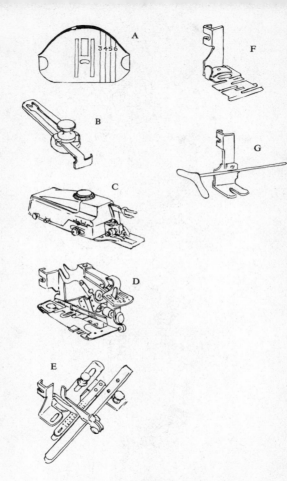

A

F

B

C

G

D

E

110

Special attachments include:

A **General-purpose throat plate**—designed with a wide hole to accommodate the side-to-side motion of zig-zag and automatic stitching. Most of the new throat plates have seam guide markings for accurate stitching.

B **Seam guide**—designed to provide an accurate stitching guide for seams and top-stitching.

C **Buttonholer**—designed to make accurate, long-lasting buttonholes on all kinds of fabrics. It has templates or patterns for making different kinds and sizes of button-holes.

D **Ruffler**—designed to make uniform gathered or pleated ruffles. Some rufflers also attach them in one process.

E **Tucker**—designed to make perfectly spaced tucks from ⅛″ to 1″ wide.

F **Edge-stitcher**—designed with five slots to guide stitching accurately. It is used to make French seams, piped edges, and lace insertions or to sew bands to lace together.

G **Quilter**—designed with a short, open foot and an adjustable space guide to allow accurate quilting in block, floral, or stroll designs.

Zigzagger or decorator—designed to permit a wide variety of decorative stitches.

Needles, Bobbins, and Tools

Extra needles and bobbins and machine tools; these are the "necessaries" smart sewers always keep on hand.

Machine needles range in size from 9—for delicate fabrics —to 18—for heavyweight fabrics.

Extra bobbins prewound with the colors you use most

often can be a great time-saver. And don't forget to keep a supply of empty bobbins on hand to avoid having to wind one color thread over another.

A small lint-removing brush, a tiny screwdriver, and sewing machine oil will help to keep your machine in top working condition.

The Measurers

Accurate fit means accurate measuring—and the following measurers should be part of your sewing equipment:

A **Tapemeasures**—the indispensable measurer. They should be 60″ long, with metal tips, of nonstretch material like fiber glass or plastic, and clearly printed on both sides.

B **Yardsticks**—for checking grain lines, among other marking uses. They should be shellacked hardwood or metal, with smooth edges to prevent snagging or catching.

C **Rulers**—in several lengths. The best, for sewing purposes, are the plastic see-through variety.

D **T-square**—in a convenient 9″ by 4″ T-form, is an excellent device for straightening grain, locating opposite grains, and altering patterns.

E **Skirt marker**—the quickest, easiest, and most accurate way to mark hems. Skirt markers are available that mark with chalk, with pins, or with a combination of both. Whichever you choose, make sure the base is heavy enough to keep the marker steady.

Other measurers that are nice to have include hem gauges, multi-purpose gauges, 6″ metal gauges.

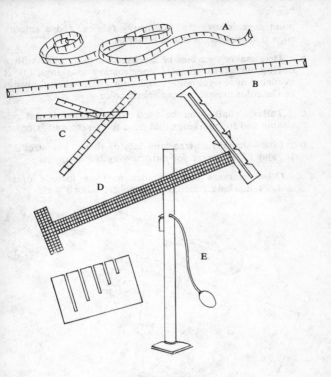

The Markers

How do you transfer pattern markings to your fabric? With any of the following markers:

A **Tracing wheels**—are available in several types. A dull, serrated edge works best for most fabrics, but a needle-

113

point edge is suggested for heavy fabrics, and a smooth edge is suggested for delicate fabrics.

_ B _ **Dressmaker's carbon or tracing paper**—is used with a tracing wheel to transfer construction markings. It is available in several colors, and your choice should always be the color closest to your fabric color.

_ C _ **Tailor's chalk**—can be used when carbon is not advisable and for markings that need to be removed later.

_ D _ **Pins**—sharp, rust-free, and lots of them. Pin sizes 15, 16, and 17 will serve for most sewing requirements.

____ **Other markers** that are nice to have include dressmaker's marking pencil, tailor tacker, tailor's wax.

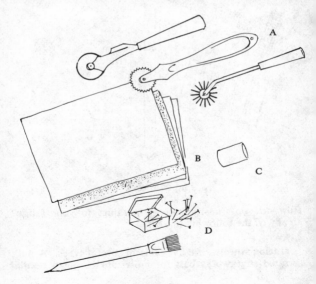

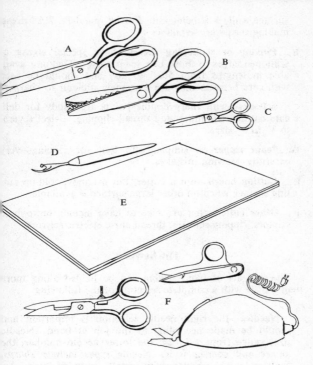

The Cutters

Accurate measuring and accurate marking need the final skill of accurate cutting. Hot drop-forged steel makes the finest, sharpest edges for the following cutters:

A **Dressmaking shears**—are 6½" to 8" bent-handle shears angled so that the fabric can rest flat on the cutting

surface while it is being cut. For left-handers, 7½" dress
making shears are available.

B — **Pinking or scalloping shears**—have special zigzag o
scalloped edges to finish raw seam edges. They are avail
able in lengths from 5½" to 10" and should be use
with care because they are extremely difficult to sharpen

C — **Scissors**—with sharp double points are handy for deli
cate cutting, trimming, and thread-clipping. Select severa
in 3" to 6" sizes.

D — **Seam ripper**—a simple, safe tool for ripping—ver
carefully—sewing mistakes.

E — **Cutting board**—not a cutter, but a handy, fold-up cut
ting surface when no other large surface is available.

F — **Other cutters** that are nice to have include buttonhol
scissors, ripping scissors, thread clips, electric scissors.

The Sewers

The fine art of hand sewing can be helped along more
than a little with a complete selection of the following:

Needles—the right needle selection is important and
should be made according to the job at hand. Needle
sizes range from 1 to 24; the lower needle number, the
longer and coarser it is. Needle types include *sharps,*
medium-length needles with small, rounded eyes; *betweens,* shorter needles with small, rounded eyes; *embroidery,* medium-length needles with long, larger eyes;
milliner's, long needles with small, rounded eyes.

Special-purpose needles include *calyx-eye* needles with
open-eye top for easy threading; *tapestry* needles for
needlepoint, petit point, and tapestry work; *cotton darners*
and *yarn darners* with long or large eyes for darning;

116

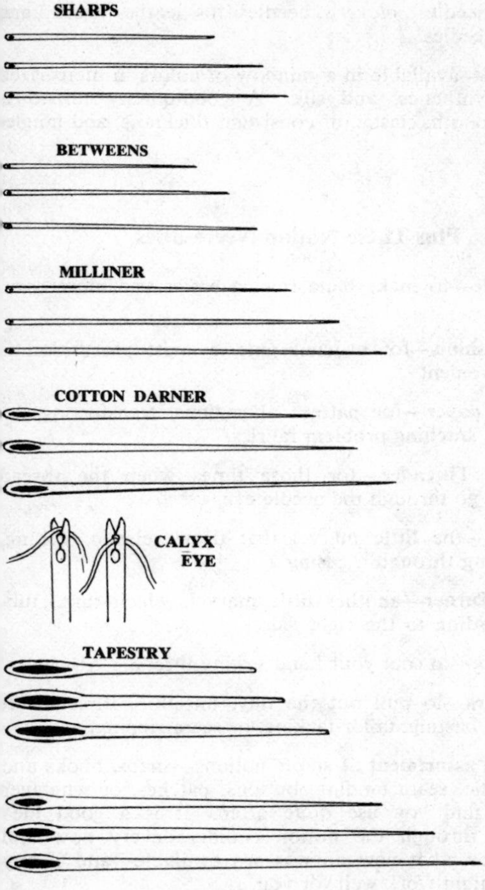

SHARPS

BETWEENS

MILLINER

COTTON DARNER

CALYX EYE

TAPESTRY

117

beading needles; *glover's* needles for leather work; and *quilting* needles.

Thread—available in a rainbow of colors in mercerized cotton, synthetics, and silk. A good-quality thread is strong, smooth, elastic, of consistent thickness, and tangle-resistant.

Plus These Notion Necessaries

Thimble—to make hand sewing easier and more comfortable.

Pin cushion—for at-hand pins, a wrist pincushion is most convenient.

Tissue paper—for pattern alterations, transferring designs, and stitching problem fabrics.

Needle Threader—for those times when the thread refuses to go through the needle eye.

Bodkin—the little marvel that draws elastic, belting, and cording through a casing.

Loop Turner—another little marvel, which turns tubing or cording to the right side.

Beeswax—to coat your hand sewing thread.

Tweezers—to pull out the tiny, unsightly threads left behind by basting, tailor tacking, or seam ripping.

And an assortment of staple notions—snaps, hooks and eyes, elastic, seam binding, buttons, patches, or whatever else you find you use quite often. It is a good idea to check through the notion counters every now and then to see what new notions are available—and if any of them might work well for you.

Needle and Thread Charts

For Machine Sewing:

Fabric Type	Threads	Machine Needle Sizes	Stitch Length Setting
Very Light: net, marquisette, chiffon, fine lace, silk organdy, organza, gossamer silks, voile, ninon	For Natural Fibers: Fine mercerized, Silk A For Synthetics: Polyspun, Poly-Bond, Nymo	Finest: 9, 11	15 to 20
Light: lawn, dimity, batiste, silk, voile, paper taffeta, sheer crepe, organdy, silk jersey, ciré, dotted Swiss, chambray	For Natural Fibers: mercerized #50, Silk A For Synthetics: Polyspun, Poly-Bond, Nymo	Fine: 11	12 to 16
Medium Light: gingham, challis, surah, satin, taffeta, sheer wool crepe, peau de soie, pongee, raw silk	For Natural Fibers: mercerized #50, Silk A For Synthetics: Polyspun, Poly-Bond, Nymo	Fine: 11, 14	12 to 15
Medium: Flannel, velvet, shantung, piqué, corduroy, broadcloth, linen, wool double knits, bonded fabrics, poplin, stretch fabrics, muslin, chintz, faille, moiré, serge, silk-and-worsted, ottoman	For Natural Fibers: mercerized #50 Silk A For Synthetics: Polyspun, Poly-Bond, Nymo	Medium: 14	12

119

Medium Heavy: denim, terry, burlap, gabardine, felt, fleece, twill, brocade, fake fur, suiting, bengaline, stretch fabrics, tweed	For Natural Fibers: mercerized #40 Silk A For Synthetics: Polyspun, PolyBond, Nymo	Medium coarse: 14, 16	10 to 1
Heavy: overcoatings, ticking, sailcloth, heavy backed vinyl, corduroy, double-faced wools, drapery fabrics	For Natural Fibers: mercerized #24, #30, #40, Silk A For Synthetics: Polyspun, PolyBond, Nymo	Coarse: 16	8 to 10
Very Heavy: Canvas, duck, work denim, wide-wale corduroy, leather, suede, upholstery fabrics	For Natural Fibers: mercerized #8, #16, #20 For Synthetics: Nymo	Coarse: 16, 18	6 to 8

For Hand Sewing:	Threads	Needle Sizes
Basting	Cotton according to fabric weight, Silk A	Cotton darners, milliners, and sharps
Beading, sequins	Cotton coated with beeswax, synthetics	Beading, sharps
Buttons, buttonholes	Cotton, synthetics, Silk D	Largest type appropriate to fabric
Darning and mending	Cotton, synthetics, Silk A, mending yarn	Sharps, embroidery

mbroidery	Embroidery floss, Silk D, yarn	Yarn darner, embroidery, sharps
astenings	Cotton, synthetics, Silk D, button and carpet (for heavy fastenings)	Embroidery, sharps, betweens
athering and hirring	Cotton, synthetics, elastic, Silk A	Embroidery, sharps, betweens
uilting	Quilting or other thread, depending on the effect desired	Betweens
op-stitching	Cotton, synthetics, Silk A, Silk D for heavy effect	Betweens, sharps

Trademarks: Polyspun—Talon; Poly-Bond—Belding Corticelli; Nymo—Belding Corticelli)

CHAPTER 6

Pattern Meets Fabric— the First Steps of Creative Sewing

The exciting moment of actual fashion creation is at hand.

Everything is assembled—fabric, findings, pattern, sewing tools. You've cleared away a large, flat working surface, and a picture of your finished fashion dances tantalizingly in your mind. But hold on to that enthusiasm for just a little while longer. There are some important final preparations that must be made if that lovely picture in your mind is to become a reality.

Your Fabric—Is It Grain-Perfect?

Nothing is more important to the final fit and appearance of your fashion than the proper use of fabric grain lines.

As you remember, all woven fabrics are made from lengthwise and crosswise threads *(see chapter 4, page 77)*. These threads, along with the fabric's true bias, are your guides to achieving grain perfection.

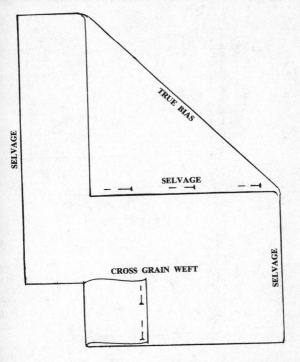

The *lengthwise grain* runs parallel to the selvage, or woven edge. It is also called the "straight of the fabric."

The *crosswise grain* runs from selvage to selvage at right angles to the lengthwise grain.

The *true bias* is the diagonal line formed by folding the fabric diagonally so the *crosswise* grain is parallel to the selvage. The maximum amount of "give" or stretchability of any fabric is found in the true bias.

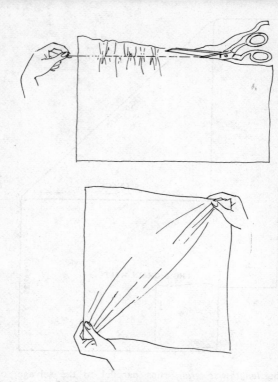

Making Your Fabric Grain-Perfect

You have wisely avoided buying a fabric that was obviously off-grain. Now you need to make sure that the lengthwise and crosswise grains of your fabric are at exact right angles to each other.

To do this, follow this step-by-step method:

124

1. Snip through one selvage edge with your scissors, about an inch or so above the end.

2. Separate and firmly grasp one crosswise thread.

3. Pull the thread gently, letting the fabric gather as you pull. Pull the thread from selvage to selvage.

4. Cut carefully along the line made by the pulled thread.

5. Fold the fabric in half lengthwise, right sides together, matching the selvages accurately.

6. If the crosswise ends you have just trimmed match evenly, your fabric is grain-perfect.

"But My Fabric Is Still Off-Grain"

If your fabric is slightly off-grain, try this. With fabric till folded lengthwise with selvage edges pinned together, gently steam-press to urge the threads into perfect position.

If your fabric is very much off-grain, try this. Pull the fabric along the true bias in the opposite direction from which the ends slant. Continue pulling until a perfect right-angle corner can be formed.

And, if your fabric is still off-grain—and washable—try this. Fold the fabric and place it in warm water for a few minutes. Pull the fabric along the true bias, as above, until a perfect right-angle corner can be formed. Hang the fabric over a clothesline or shower rack until it is completely dry. Then press smooth, being careful not to press in the fold line.

Any one—or combination—of these techniques should be enough to let you straighten your fabric. If nothing works, however, and your fabric is still badly off-grain, no amount of sewing skill will make your fashion hang right. So perhaps the best thing to do is chalk it up to experience—and remember to double-check fabric carefully *before* you buy again.

After Straightening—Preshrink

The next step in fabric preparation is preshrinking, unle$
your fabric has been preshrunk by the manufacturer or ha
been processed to prevent shrinking.

Preshrink *cottons and other washable fabrics* by using th
same method you used to damp-straighten grain, excep
this time, use hot water instead of warm water and leav
the fabric in the water for about an hour.

Woolen fabrics should be shrunk by a dry cleaner, if a
all possible, unless they are marked "presponged" or "read
for the needle."

If you prefer to do it yourself, straighten the fabric end$
snip the selvages at intervals, and fold in half lengthwise
Baste across the fabric ends and along the selvages. Plac

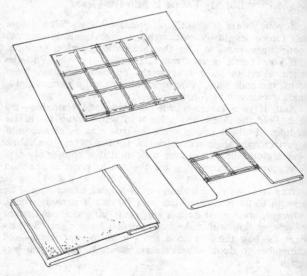

very damp sheet on a flat surface, making sure the sheet
is been smoothed to remove all wrinkles. Lay the fabric
n the sheet and carefully fold up sheet ends over the
bric. Fold fabric and sheet wrapping carefully, keeping
e sheet on the outside. Place a towel over the folded
eet so the top section doesn't dry too quickly and leave
vernight. Then unfold, smooth, and stretch the fabric into
ape and on grain. When the fabric is dry, press lightly
ith a steam iron.

Woven interfacings, linings, and underlinings should also
e checked carefully for shrinkage—and preshrunk if neces-
ry—before cutting.

Preparing Your Pattern for Cutting

Your pattern has been altered and customized to your
act measurements *(see chapter 3)*. And now you're on
ur way.

Circle the cutting layout appropriate to your size, fabric
nap, and fabric width. If your pattern selection calls for
lining, interfacing, or contrasting fabric, circle those layouts, too.

**Select the pattern pieces indicated for the version you
are making** and tuck all other pattern pieces safely back
in the envelope. You may want them for a later fashion
venture. And, just to be sure, check each pattern piece
selected and make certain it is marked with the same
size and pattern number.

Press each pattern piece with a dry iron set at lowest
temperature.

**Fold your prepared fabric according to the layout
diagram.** Fold carefully along a single thread with right
sides together, unless you must match a pattern visible

127

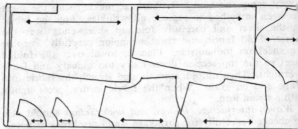

only on the right side. Pin the fabric together every three inches or so along all ends and selvages. If necessary clip the selvage so that the fabric lies flat.

Pin the pattern to the fabric according to the layout shown on the diagram, being mindful of pattern fold lines and lengthwise grain lines. And always—*always*—lay out the entire pattern before cutting.

Pinning and Cutting the Professional Way

There's something terribly final about cutting into your fabric. A cutting mistake, unlike a badly sewn seam, cannot be ripped out. But that instant of nervousness before you cut can be eased considerably if you follow these pinning and cutting suggestions carefully.

Pattern Cutting Guide

- Lay out all pattern pieces before you begin cutting.
- Use "with nap" layouts whenever necessary and for uneven stripes, plaids, and prints.
- Place all pattern pieces printed side up unless otherwise indicated by your cutting guide.

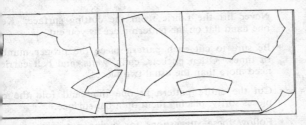

- With pencil and ruler, continue grain lines to pattern ends.

- Pin first along fold lines and lengthwise grain lines.

- Measure often to make sure pattern pieces are placed on the correct grain line.

- When grain lines are measured and correct, smooth out the pattern piece and pin *with* the grain of fabric and *inside* the seam allowance.

- When your layout shows a pattern piece extending beyond the fabric fold, cut the other pieces first, then unfold the fabric and cut out the remaining piece.

- Use plenty of fine, sharp pins to prevent the fabric from slipping as you cut.

- Cut in the direction of the grain to avoid distorting the fabric.

- Use bent-handle dressmaker's shears with good, sharp cutting edges. Cut with steady, even slashes.

- *Never* cut out a pattern with pinking shears. Use them only to finish seams during construction.

- Use the point of the scissors to cut notches outward. Cut groups of notches in continuous blocks for easier matching.

129

- Never lift the fabric from the cutting surface. Ke one hand flat on the pattern piece as you cut.

- Be sure to cut each pattern piece the proper numb of times. Often pockets, cuffs, welts, and belt carrie need more than the usual two pieces.

- Cut the entire pattern at one time and fold the c pieces softly, placing them on a flat surface.

- Follow these suggestions for laying out, pinning, ar cutting interfacings, linings, and contrast-fabric detail

Plaids, Checks, Stripes, and Florals— the "Problem" Fabrics

Plaids, stripes, checks, and florals: these are the "prob lem" fabrics to lay out. But you've solved some of th problems by selecting only those patterns that are suitabl for them. And you've purchased the additional yardag necessary for matching them.

Even plaids—those that have the same stripe arrang ment in both lengthwise and crosswise directions—are rela tively easy to match. Make sure the center fold line fall along the center of the plaid design. If it does not, refol until it does. And always double-check to make sure th

EVEN PLAID · UNEVEN PLAID

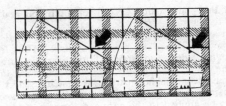

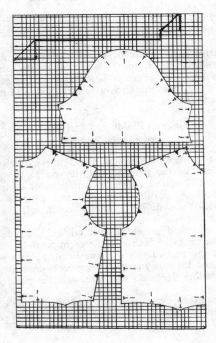

lines of the plaid match exactly on both top and botto
folds of the fabric.

The secret of matching plaids is simply this: alwa
match the seam lines, not the cutting lines. Thus front ar
back bodice side seam notches, for example, are place
along the same part of the plaid pattern. *(See diagram*
This same technique holds true for matching skirt notch
and is especially important for matching pockets or oth
details to be applied to the garment during construction.

Even stripes and checks are handled and matched th
same way as even plaids.

Even plaids and checks should match perfectly at sid
seams, center seams, shoulder seams, waistline, armhole
and sleeves.

Even stripes should match perfectly at center seams an
when possible, side seams. They should also match a
shoulder seams and where collars and yokes meet bodic
unless they are bias-cut. Crosswise stripes should match a
armholes and sleeves.

Uneven Plaids and Stripes— Not for the Novice

If you're a beginning sewer, avoid uneven striped an
plaid fabrics like the plague. But, if you have some ex
perience, and if you've chosen a pattern with as few con
struction lines as possible, the time and patience neede
to work with these difficult patterns could bring a whop
ping fashion bonus.

An uneven plaid or stripe has an unbalanced design
making matching in both directions impossible. So yo
must select the particular plaid line or stripe you want t
emphasize and lay out your pattern pieces—matching sean
lines, not cutting lines—so that your selected plaid line o
stripe corresponds.

In your concern over matching, don't forget the cardina
rule of pattern layout. *KEEP THOSE GRAIN LINE*
STRAIGHT!

132

Balancing a Pretty Print

You're striving for a final, harmonious effect when you cut a large-scale print—and you can best obtain it by laying all pattern pieces in the same direction and shifting them along the grain line until you achieve the desired harmony.

And the Other "Problem" Fabrics

They run the range from filmiest chiffon to fabulou
fake furs—and they're exciting to use provided you know
the secrets of handling them.

Turn back to *chapter 4, pages 83 to 93* for detailed in
structions for handling bonded fabrics, chiffon, fake furs
jersey and double knits, lace, laminated fabrics, silk, stretch
fabrics, velvet, velveteen, corduroy, and wash-and-wear
fabrics.

Making Your Mark

Your pattern pieces, with their tissue patterns still at
tached, are sitting in a neat pile waiting for the next step
And that is to transfer all pattern markings to the fabric—
carefully, accurately, completely.

You can use any or all of the following transfer methods:

- **Tracing wheel and carbon**—for most fabrics except
  sheers and heavy, napped fabrics. Always mark on
  the wrong side by placing dressmaker's carbon next to
  the wrong side of the fabric to be marked. Place pat
  tern piece on a flat, hard surface and mark lightly
  along transfer lines with a tracing wheel.

- **Tailor's tacks**—for any type of fabric. Use a double
  thread in a contrasting color. At the point to be
  marked, take a small stitch through the pattern and
  double thickness of fabric, leaving a short, unknotted
  end. Then, take a backstitch in the same place, leav
  ing a little loop. Clip the thread, leaving another short
  end. Gently clip threads between fabric layers and
  separate. Remove pattern tissue carefully so you don't
  pull out the tailor's tacks.

- **Tailor's chalk or chalk pencil**—for most fabrics except
  heavy, napped wools. Pin through pattern and double

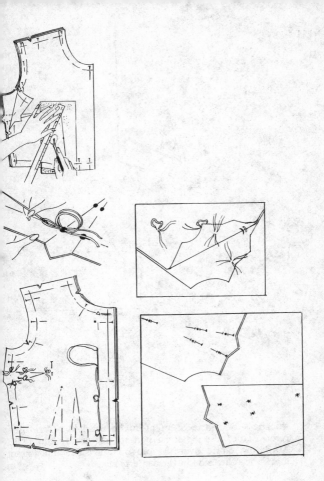

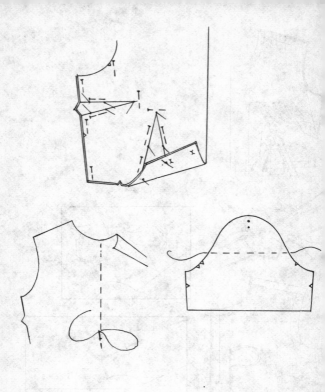

thickness of fabric at point to be marked. Carefully remove the tissue pattern without disturbing the pins. Mark the fabric over the pin on one side. Turn and mark the other side in the same place.

- **Clip marking**—for any fabric and for the experienced sewer. Using sharp shears, clip into the seam allowance carefully to mark center front and back, top and bottom of pleats, tops of darts, tucks, and fold lines.

- **Pin marking**—for most fabrics except delicate sheers. On the pattern side, drive a pin straight through pattern and double thickness of fabric. Turn and mark the other side the same way, driving the second pin through the hole made by the first. Gently remove tissue pattern without disturbing the pin and separate thicknesses. Pin markings should be basted as soon as possible.

- **Baste marking**—for every fabric, to mark center front and back and grain lines at the cap of a set-in sleeve. Baste-stitch along center folds before removing tissue pattern. Buttonholes, placement of decorative details, and pleats can be marked this way.

Stay-Stitching—the Shape-Holder

Stay-stitching is a line of machine stitching placed through a single thickness inside the seam allowance, about ½″ from the edge. Its purpose? To hold the original shape of necklines, shoulder lines, waistlines, and hip lines *before* they are basted.

Many of today's stabilized fabrics do not need to be stay-stitched. But for stretchy fabrics stay-stitching is a must.

Stay-stitch in these directions:

NECKLINE—from shoulder to center

SHOULDER—from neckline to armhole

WAISTLINE—from side seams to center

137

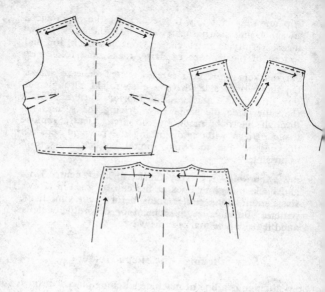

HIPLINE and bias skirt seams—from lower edge to waist-line

V NECKLINE—from point of V to shoulder

And now you're ready to put your fashion together.

CHAPTER 7

Step-By-Step Pressing—
the Professional
Touch

If there is one real secret of successful sewing, it is simply this: PRESS AS YOU SEW!

Or, to put it another way, always press a stitched seam
before it is crossed by another seam.

Or, to put it still another way, no amount of pressing
after your garment is finished will make up for the step-
by-step pressing that should be done as each sewing detail
is completed.

Pressing—Not Ironing

The art of pressing as you sew is a very specialized one
—not at all the same as the art of ironing.

When you iron, you glide your iron over the fabric to
remove wrinkles and restore the garment's original shape.

When you press, the iron barely moves over the surface
of the fabric. Instead, it remains in contact with the detail
to be pressed—seam, dart, tuck, etc.—and then is lifted
and moved on to the next area to be pressed.

Pressing Necessaries

A good steam-dry iron—the very best you can afford, with an accurate fabric dial to control temperature, is the most important pressing necessary.

An adjustable ironing board—which can be raised or lowered to conform to your height. It should be sturdy and securely covered with a smooth, durable ironing board pad and cover.

Press cloths—of cheesecloth for light- and medium-weight fabrics, of cotton canvas for wools or fabrics that can't stand much heat, of woven wool interlining for top pressing, plus any of the commercially treated press cloths.

Press mitt and tailor's ham—two essentials for pressing and shaping curved details. The press mitt is a small pocketed and padded pressing aid that slips over the hand. The tailor's ham is a firm, ham-shaped cushion that slips under curved details to facilitate pressing. Both are available commercially, but either can be made quickly and inexpensively with firm cotton and a well-packed stuffing of kapok, sawdust, or wool scraps.

Seam roll—a rolled, padded cushion that slips under the seam to be pressed and prevents ridges from forming.

Pressing pad—a make-it-yourself pressing aid for such details as zippers, corded buttonholes, pockets in napped fabrics, and monograms. Take three or four 14″ by 20″ thicknesses of wool interlining and stitch them to a backing of canvas or drill. Place under detail with backing on ironing board, interlining right side up.

Needle board—a must for pressing pile fabrics. The fabric is placed face down so the pile fits between the needles and can be pressed without matting.

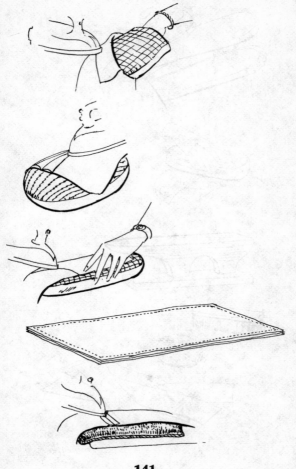

141

Sleeve board—a well-padded, short, narrow board that fits nicely on top of your ironing board and is a must for pressing sleeves, seams, and other details.

Wooden clapper and point presser—two essentials for precise tailoring. The clapper is a shaped wooden block that is pounded against a seam or edge to be steam-pressed. The point presser is a thin, shaped wooden board with a sharp point that helps to open seams in corners, points, and other difficult areas.

Plus: clothes brush to raise the nap on pile fabrics and to remove stray lint and threads; **sponge** for moistening your press cloth and mopping up any unfortunate spills, and **brown paper strips** to slip under dart folds or pleat edges to prevent ridging on the right side.

The Pressers—at Hand and Handy

Get into the habit of setting up your pressing equipment along with your sewing equipment. And make it a habit to press—carefully and properly—each construction detail after it has been stitched.

Time-consuming habits? Perhaps they are. But your final pressing will be relatively quick and easy. And you'll never again turn out a fashion that looks "home-made" because of faulty pressing. And isn't *that* worth the extra time needed for step-by-step pressing?

Know Your Fabric—and How to Press It

How will you press your fabric? That depends on its fiber content, its texture, and its thickness. Fiber content determines the proper temperature setting for your iron; texture and thickness determine the proper method of handling the fabric.

Fiber content can best be established at the time you purchase your fabric by checking the information on the bolt or on the hang tag. But if there was no fiber information available, you'll need to do a bit of testing yourself.

Check the fabric chart on *pages 78 to 82, chapter 4,* and try to identify your fabric by the characteristics listed. Then, test-press a scrap of your fabric just to make sure.

Set the dial of your iron at the lowest temperature and begin test-pressing. Increase the temperature gradually until you can press the fabric scrap smoothly and easily.

Test-pressing is a good idea, even when you know the fiber content of your fabric. And so are the following:

- Always press on the wrong side to prevent shine.
- Always use a press cloth—except for cottons and linens —to supply sufficient moisture. The steam from your iron isn't always enough.
- Always lift fabric with both hands when it needs to be moved.
- Always press in the direction of the fabric grain. This is especially important if you are pressing a bias-cut section.
- Always keep the bottom of your iron clean.

Do not overpress. Overpressing can happen if you apply too much moisture, use a too-hot iron (see below for recommended pressing temperatures), leave the iron in one place too long, use the wrong press cloth, or go over the same spot too often.

The "How-to's" of Fabric Pressing

Press at lowest temperature setting for *acetates, acrylics, and nylons.* Press on wrong side, using a thin press cloth. If steam is needed—the iron temperature is not high enough to create steam—use a moist press cloth over the dry press cloth.

144

Press at slightly higher temperature setting for *rayons and polyesters*. Press on the wrong side, using a thin press cloth. In most cases, the iron temperature is high enough to create sufficient steam. If additional steam is needed, especially along seams, use a moist press cloth over the dry press cloth.

Press at medium temperature setting for *silk,* but be careful, because too hot an iron will weaken the fiber and cause discoloration. Press on the wrong side, using a thin press cloth. Silk has a tendency to water-spot so, if additional moisture is necessary, use a moist press cloth over a dry press cloth.

Press at slightly higher temperature setting for *lightweight cotton*. Press on wrong side directly on the fabric. If the cotton is dark in color, use a moist press cloth and press dry. A moist press cloth is also helpful in pressing seams, darts, and other construction details.

Press at high temperature setting for *wool*. Press on the wrong side, using a heavy press cloth. It is important to use sufficient moisture to press wool properly. If enough moisture is not produced by the iron, use a moist press cloth over the dry press cloth. *Never press wool when it is wet:* the fabric will shrink and lose its elasticity. *Never press wool completely dry:* the fabric will produce a shine. If the wool has a slight nap, brush while there is still moist steam. If the wool has a deeper nap, press over a needle board.

Press at highest temperature setting for *linen and heavyweight cotton*. Press on wrong side directly on the fabric. If the fabric is dark in color, use a moist press cloth and press dry. Use additional moisture along seams to prevent them from puckering.

Steam-press high-pile fabrics like *velvet, velveteen, and corduroy* on a needle board to prevent them from matting down. Place the fabric face down on the needle board.

Hold the steam iron close to the fabric—not on it—and brush the iron lightly across the fabric to distribute steam. Press open seams with your fingertips, but be careful not to fingermark the fabric. Lift the fabric only after it is completely dry.

Steam-press *laminated fabrics* during construction and never let the iron come into contact with the foam backing. The final pressing should be done on the right side over a press cloth.

Set temperature according to heat required for the most delicate fiber in a *fabric blend*. For a wool and acrylic blend, for example, set your iron temperature low, for acrylic, rather than high, for wool.

Set temperature according to heat required for *lace and embroidered fabrics*. Press on the wrong side after placing fabric over several layers of toweling. This prevents the design from being flattened down.

The "How-to's" of Construction Pressing

Before you begin your construction pressing, remember to remove all pins and basting stitches. Pressed-over pins leave marks in the fabric and often mar the soleplate of your iron. Basting stitches also leave an imprint on the fabric.

However, if you must leave basting stitches in the fabric, be sure to use silk basting thread and a diagonal basting stitch *(see page 150)*.

Press **seams** over a sleeve board or a seam roll in the same direction as they were stitched. Hold the seam allowances open with your fingers and press with the point of the iron along the stitching line. If the fabric is heavy, slip strips of brown paper between the seam allowance and the body of the garment. This will help to avoid ridge marks on the right side of the fabric.

Press **curved seams** over a press mitt or tailor's ham, following the same techniques as for a straight seam.

Press **French seams** with the point of the iron as carefully as possible to avoid pressing a shine into the fabric. After trimming the seam allowance and turning to the wrong side, fold and press again on the wrong side. Complete your final pressing after the seam has been stitched on the wrong side.

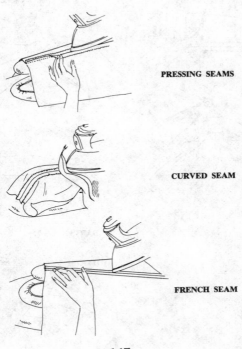

PRESSING SEAMS

CURVED SEAM

FRENCH SEAM

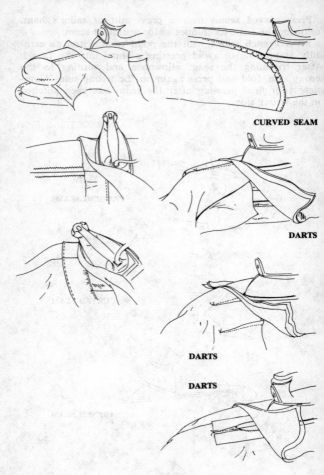

CURVED SEAM

DARTS

DARTS

DARTS

Press **lapped seam** on the wrong side after the edge has been folded under and basted. Press again after the seam is lapped and stitched. If top pressing is needed, use a press cloth.

Press **darts** flat, as they were stitched, carrying the crease only as far as the line of stitching. Shrink out fullness at the point of the dart. Vertical darts, like those at the waistline or shoulder, are usually pressed toward the center front or center back. Horizontal darts, like bust and elbow darts, are usually pressed down. Darts in heavy fabrics should be slashed and pressed open. If necessary, place strips of brown paper between slashed dart allowances and the body of the garment to prevent ridging.

Press **tucks** in the same direction as they were stitched, making sure not to press beyond the line of stitching. Then press them in the direction where they will lie.

Press **gathers** by moving the point of the iron up toward the stitching. Be careful to smooth out the fabric below the iron so creases will not form. Never place the iron flat across the gathering stitches. They will be creased and flattened and will lose the soft effect of gathering. If two gathered edges are stitched together, use a seam roll to open seam allowances.

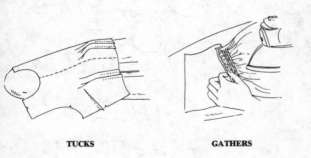

TUCKS   GATHERS

Press **sleeves** *after* they have been pin-fitted into armholes and proper amount of ease has been drawn. When the pin-fitting is satisfactory, remove sleeve and place cap over the press mitt or tailor's ham. Cover cap seam allowance with a press cloth and, with moisture, carefully shrink out the fullness. Use the point of the iron and be careful not to press beyond the line of stitching. After the sleeve is stitched into the armhole, press again, this time using the end of the sleeve board. Press on the wrong side with a press cloth, and press *only* the seam allowance. Turn the seam allowance into the sleeve without any additional pressing.

Press **lower edge** of the sleeve on the right side only. Press over a sleeve board to retain the circular shape.

Press **facing seams** in the same direction as they were stitched. Press after seams have been trimmed, graded, and slashed where necessary. Place the seam over a seam roll and press open with the point of the iron. Apply moisture as necessary with a sponge or brush. After the facing seam has been pressed open, turn facing inside and press again, using press cloth and necessary moisture. This double pressing should give the facing seam a flatter finish.

Press **plackets** over a tailor's ham or the small end of a sleeve board. Make sure the zipper is closed; then press on the right side with a press cloth. Don't try to press over the metal zipper pull. Instead, pull down zipper, reset press cloth, and press the top of the placket.

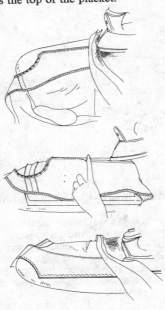

Press **hem** first *after* it has been marked but *before* it has been stitched. Place garment, wrong side up, over the end of the ironing board. Turn up the hem as marked, cover with press cloth, and press carefully. Pick up the iron after you have pressed each section and go on to the next section. Press again after the hem has been trimmed. If the skirt is gored or flared, there will be additional fullness in the hem. Stitch a gathering thread about ½″ from the top of the hem and, matching seams, draw the thread until the hem fits smoothly. Use a damp press cloth to shrink out gathering fullness. After the final hemming, press again on the wrong side, using a press cloth and the necessary amount of moisture.

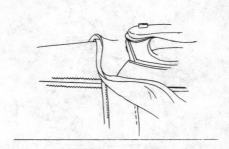

And Finally—the Final Pressing

You have pressed each and every construction detail with great care as you sewed. And now, your final pressing should be simply a matter of removing wrinkles here and there or touching up an occasional edge.

By following the step-by-step ironing method, you've banished the "home-made" look—and your new fashion is ready to be worn proudly.

CHAPTER 8

Putting It All Together—Fashion Construction from A to Z

How do those flat pieces of fabric you've cut and marked so carefully become a well-shaped, perfectly fitted fashion? By putting them together, step by step, according to the instructions printed on your pattern sewing guide.

But no pattern sewing guide, not even the most detailed one, can cover all you need to know to make your garment a complete success.

There are, of course, many ways to achieve a satisfactory result in fashion construction, many ways to finish a seam or hem a skirt. Your own sewing skill, experience, creativity, and temperament will dictate many of them.

This chapter, arranged alphabetically according to fashion construction processes from *assembling* a garment to sewing in a *zipper*, will *augment* your pattern sewing guide.

The construction processes described in this chapter have

been selected because they are up-to-date; because they save time and error; because they work.

As your fashion begins to take shape, you may want to double-check a particular sewing process before you begin it. Simply turn to the proper listing, skim through the suggested method, and put your new knowledge to work for you.

ASSEMBLING A GARMENT

Organize your work if you want to save time, effort, and costly mistakes.

And the best way to organize is to assemble your garment according to the unit construction method. Simply explained, *unit construction* means to complete as much work as possible on each garment unit before attaching it to the next unit.

If you are making a dress, for example, you complete the skirt front first, attaching pockets if called for. Then you complete the skirt back. Then you attach skirt front and back, leaving zipper edges open.

The bodice is assembled in the same way—sleeves, in-

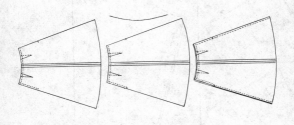

cluding cuffs, finished first; facing prepared; collar completed; bodice front interfaced and all details like button holes and yokes, completed; bodice back interfaced and completed; bodice front and back joined at shoulders; collar and facing attached and side seams stitched; sleeves set in . . . and, finally, skirt and bodice joined and zipper and finishing touches applied.

Study your own pattern carefully to determine what is necessary to complete a particular unit, and proceed accordingly.

BASTING

Basting is temporary stitching, by hand or by machine, with long, loose stitches that are removed after the job is finished.

Or you may pin-baste—use pins to secure several layers of fabric—in preparation for thread-basting or instead of thread-basting.

To pin-baste: As a preliminary to thread-basting or stitching, place pins at right angles to fabric edge within seam allowances. Match all notches and seam ends as you

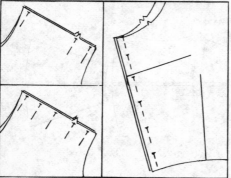

PIN-BASTING

156

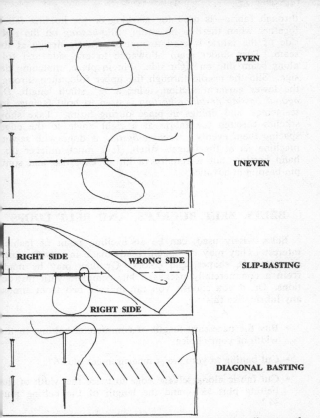

EVEN

UNEVEN

RIGHT SIDE

WRONG SIDE

SLIP-BASTING

RIGHT SIDE

DIAGONAL BASTING

pin. As a preliminary to pin-fitting, pin on seamline parallel to fabric edge on the *right side* of the garment.

To thread-baste by hand: Take even stitches about ¼″ apart. *Uneven basting*—long stitches on top, short stitches through fabric—is used for marking or for holding fabric together when there is no strain. *Slip-basting* on the right side of the fabric is used to match a fabric design at the seam. Turn under seam allowance to one side and fold along seam line on right side. Pin in place, matching design. Slip the needle through the upper fold, then through the lower garment section, using a ½" stitch length. *Diagonal basting or tailor basting* is used to hold facings, interfacings, and linings in place during fitting. Take short stitches through the fabric at a right angle to the edge, spacing them evenly. *Machine-basting* is done with sewing machine set at the longest stitch. It is much quicker than hand basting, but it requires a bit of expertise and some pin-basting in advance.

BELTS, BELT BUCKLES, AND BELT LOOPS

Belts, wisely used, can be an exciting point of fashion interest. They may be bought ready-made in a wide range of materials, shapes, and colors. Or they may be made from a commercially packaged kit, complete with instructions. Or, if you choose, you can make a belt from almost any fabric, like this:

- Buy the necessary length of commercial belting, in the width of your choice.

- Cut belting to your waist measurement plus 6".

- Cut fabric along selvage edge to twice the width of the belting plus ½"—and the length of the belting plus ¾".

- Carefully measure and cut a point at one end of the belting. Be sure cut angles are exactly equal.

- Fold fabric strip in half lengthwise with right sides

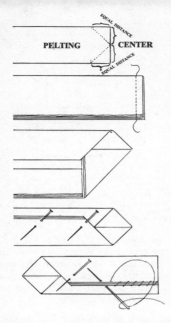

together and stitch as shown. Trim seam, press open, and turn.

- Open lengthwise fold, causing stitched end to form a point.

- Slip pointed end of belting inside fabric point, fold fabric along grain line over belting top and bottom, and press.

- With selvage edge overlapping cut edge, slipstitch. Trim away excess fabric beyond ¼″ of belting at straight edge.

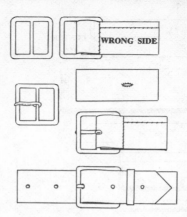

- Attach buckle, as follows. If buckle has no prong, fold straight edge over buckle bar and sew down. If buckle has a prong, cut a ½″ horizontal slot starting 1½″ from straight end of belt. Overcast raw edge of slot, slip belt prong through, fold belt end to wrong side around buckle bar, and slipstitch.

- Try on belt and mark point where belt prong should come through comfortably. Mark two more points on each side at 1″ distances. Make eyelets, and finish by hand with buttonhole stitch or with metal eyelets.

- *Note:* If a belt loop is desired, it must be made and slipped into position *before* straight end at buckle is slipstitched.

Making a belt loop: Belt loops or carriers are necessary to keep a belt firmly in place. For belt loops made of thread, *see* **THREAD LOOPS.** Make fabric loops as follows:

- Cut a strip of fabric along selvage edge long enough for the number of belt loops needed. Each loop needs the width of the belt plus 1″. The width of the fabric strip is determined by the width desired for the finished belt loop.

- Fold raw edge lengthwise to the inside and press. Fold selvage edge over it and press.

- Top-stitch along both folded edges. If you prefer, slip-stitch by hand. Cut strip into single loop lengths.

- Place belt loops on garment where needed—remember to center over belt line. Fold under raw edges top and bottom ¼″ and top-stitch by machine or slipstitch by hand.

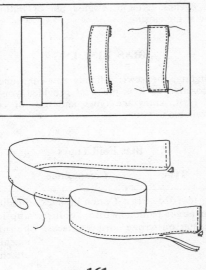

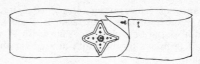

Variations on the Belt Theme

Making a tie belt or sash: Cut fabric—bias, straight grain, wide or narrow, the choice is yours—twice the width desired plus seam allowances, and long enough to tie. Fold in half lengthwise, right sides together. Stitch the ends and long edge, leaving a small opening for turning. Trim corners and seam allowance, turn, and press. Slipstitch the opening.

Making a trimmed belt: Make a straight belt as directed and fasten it with hooks and eyes instead of a buckle. Do not make eyelets. Add a jeweled pin or button or self-fabric bow at the closing.

BIAS BINDING

Bias binding, the sewer's handy raw-edge encloser, can be as decorative as it is practical provided you handle it properly. First, know the types and uses of commercial binding available to you.

Bias Fold Tapes

Width	Type	Composition	Uses
½"	Single-fold bias tape, edges folded to center on wrong side.	Cotton in black, white, colors, stripes, checks.	Binding, facing, appliqué. Can be used with machine binder attachment.

¼"	Double-fold bias tape, same as single-fold plus extra fold just off center.	Cotton in black, white, colors.	Extra-quick binding, appliqué.
1"	Quilt-binding wide bias tape, edges folded ¼" to wrong side.	Cotton in black, white, colors.	Facing, binding.
2"	Bias hem facing, edges folded ¼" to wrong side.	Cotton in black, white, colors. Rayon in black, white, colors.	Facing, binding.
¼"	Corded piping with ⅛" seam allowance.	Cotton in black, white, colors.	Piping.

Or make your own bias binding like this:

- Find the true grain of the fabric to be cut into bias strips *(see chapter 6, page 122).*

- Mark the desired width of strip with a yardstick and mark as many strips as necessary, allowing 1" for every joining necessary and 4" for a final joining.

- Cut strips and join by placing right sides together *at right angles.* Let points extend so that edges cross at seamline, forming small angles.

- Stitch along straight grain. Press open and trim to ¼".

- Stretch your bias strip by pressing firmly with one hand while stretching strip with the other hand. Press into curve if necessary.

163

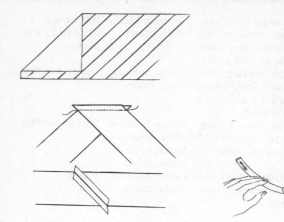

To Apply Bias Binding:

- Trim seam allowance from edges to be bound. Pre-shape your bias strip as described above to match any curved edges.

- Open out bias strip and, with right sides and raw edges together, pin bias to edge of garment.

- Baste, placing stitches within the finished width of the binding.

- Stitch next to but not on the basting so it can be removed easily.

- Turn bias over the seam allowance. Pin and slipstitch on the wrong side.
  Use this method for both commercial and hand-cut bias binding.

164

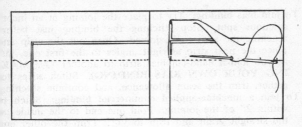

or speedy, machine-applied commercial binding:

- Follow procedure for trimming seam allowance and preshaping bias strip.

- With garment right side up, slip edge to be bound between double-fold bias tape, making sure narrower fold is on top.

- Top-stitch. The wider bottom fold will be stitched through automatically.

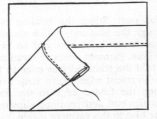

When bias binding is used as a trim, special care should be taken in the difficult areas—inside and outside corners, joinings, and endings. The following hints for handling these difficult areas should be helpful.

To join bias binding: Try to place the joining in an inconspicuous spot. Stop stitching the binding just before reaching the area to be joined. Open out the strip and place the next strip at right angles to the first one, just as you join a hand-cut bias strip to another (*see* **MAKING YOUR OWN BIAS BINDING**). Stitch strips together, trim the seam allowance, and continue stitching.

To join a machine-applied commercial binding: Stitch to within 2″ of the joining. Fold one end to the inside on the straight grain and trim to ¼″. Trim the other end the same way, but do not fold under. Pin folded edge over trimmed edge and stitch across the joining. The joining may be slipstitched if desired.

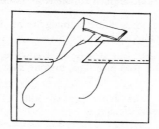

To finish a bias end: Stitch the binding beyond garment end and through the bias end, which should extend about 1″ beyond garment. Trim bias end to ¼″ beyond garment edge. Trim garment seam allowance at a diagonal at edge and fold the trimmed bias edge to the inside until it ends at the garment edge. Turn strip over seam allowance, matching the folded edge to the line of stitching. Slipstitch the bias end and continue slipstitching the folded edge of the bias to the garment inside.

To turn an outside corner: Stitch binding toward corner, stopping at width of seam allowance from corner. Remove garment, cut thread, and secure ends. Fold strip according to diagram and begin sewing again as shown.

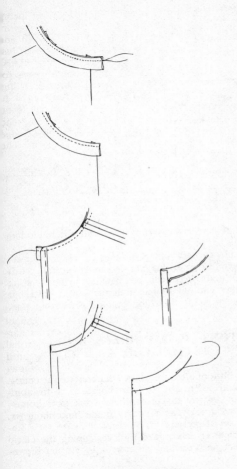

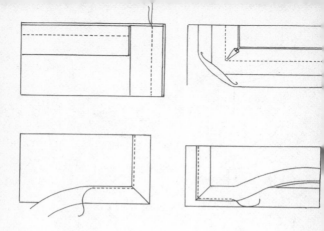

Form miter at corner on wrong side. Slipstitch binding on wrong side.

To turn an inside corner: Stitch binding to width of seam allowance beyond corner, leaving needle in garment. Lift presser foot, pivot garment on needle, bring binding around corner, and continue stitching. Form miter at corner on wrong side. Slipstitch binding on wrong side.

BUTTONS, BUTTONHOLES, AND BUTTON LOOPS

Buttons and buttonholes are more than mere fasteners. They can be, and often are, the "making" of a fashion. And nothing can destroy the professional look of a home-created fashion as quickly as a poorly made buttonhole or a poorly chosen set of buttons.

Button placement is determined by overlapping the clos-ing to the correct position and pinning it in place. Slip a

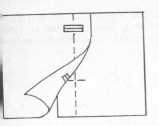

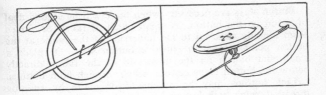

pin through each buttonhole near the end closest to the garment edge. Separate the closure and secure the pin. The center of the button should be located at the point marked by the pin.

Sew-through buttons need a thread shank to allow the fabric to lie smoothly around the button. The length of the shank should equal the thickness of the garment at the buttonhole plus ⅛″ for movement. Slip a pin or toothpick over the button and sew *over* it while you attach button. Remove pin or toothpick, raise the button to the top of the stitches, and wind thread tightly around slack *under* button to form the thread shank.

Shank buttons have thin metal shanks and do not need thread shanks. Attach by making small stitches at right angles to the buttonhole so the metal shank does not spread open the buttonhole.

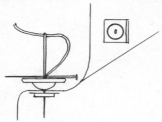

Button stays are necessary when there will be a good deal of strain on the button. A small patch of fabric or woven seam binding attached to the underside of the fabric at the button point makes an effective button stay. Or place a small, flat button on the underside of the fabric directly below the button to be sewed. Stitch through both buttons.

Link buttons may be purchased or made by running thread through both buttons several times, keeping buttons separated the desired amount. Work over the thread link with a blanket stitch (*see* **HAND STITCHES**) and secure thread.

Rough-edged buttons that may fray the buttonhole are best attached by sewing them directly to the buttonhole and sewing a series of snaps along the closing. The effect will be that of a regular buttonhole closing without any danger from snagging.

Self-fabric buttons can be made from a kit or by using bone or plastic rings as a base. Cut fabric circles twice the diameter of the rings. Gather outside edges with doubled thread. Draw up over ring and fasten securely. To trim, take stitches inside ring in the decorative pattern of your choice. To finish, cover the back with a small circle of fabric.

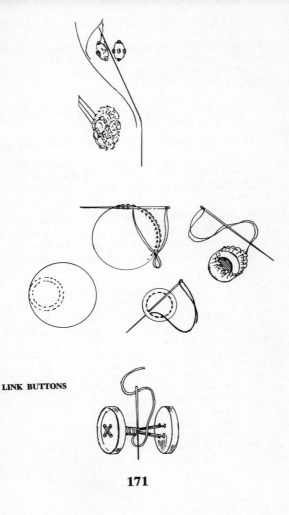

LINK BUTTONS

171

Making Buttonholes

Buttonholes may be bound with fabric or worked with thread by hand or by machine. But no matter what method you choose, the following suggestions will help you to achieve perfect buttonholes each time.

- Keep a pair of scissors with very sharp points and a 6″ ruler on hand.

- Have your buttons on hand as you mark your pattern

- Practice, *practice,* PRACTICE . . . using scraps of the actual fabric plus any interlining that will be part of the final garment where the buttonholes are to be placed.

- If you have altered your pattern, respace the buttonholes before marking and mark according to the actual size of the buttons. Make sure buttonhole markings are grain-perfect, either horizontally or vertically.

Making Bound Buttonholes

By the one-piece method: Cut a strip of self-fabric about 1″ wide and 1″ longer than the buttonhole. On wrong side of strip, baste-mark the lengthwise center accurately. With wrong sides together, fold edges up so they meet at the center marking, and press lightly. Baste center of strip to buttonhole marking on right side with cut edges of strip up. Machine-stitch with small stitches ⅛″ above and below center and across ends. (It is helpful to count the number of stitches taken across ends to keep buttonholes uniform.) Overlap stitches where you began. Slash carefully at center and then diagonally to each corner. Turn strip to the inside and press. The folded edges should form even bindings along each side and meet at the center of the opening.

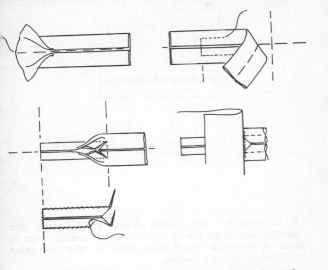

Catchstitch triangular ends to ends of binding strip to form strong square corners.

After the facing has been applied, secure it in place around buttonholes with pins. Slash the facing carefully, within the outline of the buttonhole. Turn raw edges under and hem in place.

By the two-piece method: Cut two strips of self-fabric about ½" wide and 1" longer than the buttonhole. Fold each strip in half lengthwise, wrong sides together, and press. Stitch close to the raw edge. Place the strips on right side of the garment, with raw edges along buttonhole marking. Stitch between buttonhole edge markings and ⅛" from raw edges. *Do not stitch across ends.* Slash carefully at center and then diagonally to corners. Turn strips to wrong sides; catchstitch triangular ends to ends of binding strips. Finish through facing as described above.

173

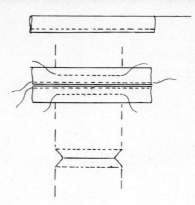

To add cording: Slip cording through binding strips with a tapestry needle or tubing turner before turning strips to inside. A one-piece bound buttonhole can also be corded by following the same method.

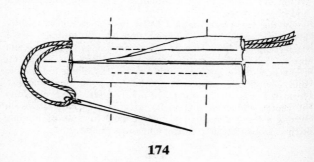

Making a Machine-Worked Buttonhole

If your machine is equipped for zigzag sewing or if you have a buttonhole attachment, follow the manual instructions carefully. And always test-sew a buttonhole on scrap fabric first.

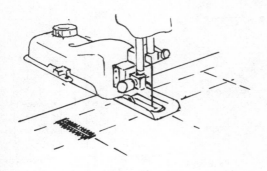

Making a Hand-Worked Buttonhole

These buttonholes are made after the facing is applied. Machine-stitch a scant ⅛" on either side and across both ends of buttonhole marking. Carefully slash along the lengthwise marking. Take an 18" length of buttonhole twist and insert needle at one end. Anchor the thread with backstitches on the wrong side. Work the buttonhole stitch from right to left, needle pointing toward you, as illustrated. Fan out stitches at the end closest to the finished edge as shown. Finish with a bar tack by taking one or more stitches across the straight end of the buttonhole and working over these threads with a blanket stitch.

175

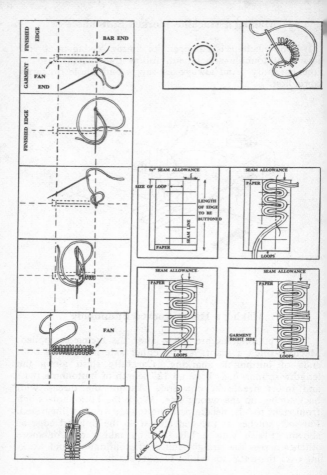

176

Making a Hand-Worked Eyelet

Cut a small circle in the fabric the size of the eyelet. Baste around hole as a reinforcement. Work over edge with a buttonhole stitch or a blanket stitch (*see* **HAND STITCHES**).

Making a Button Loop

On a faced edge, loops are applied before the facing is attached. Loops can be made of round braid, packaged cording, or self-covered cording (*see* **CORDING**).

Cut a piece of heavy paper about 2″ wide and the length of the opening. Mark off the seam allowance along one edge of the paper. Form loops of the size needed and place them on paper as shown. Place paper and first end of cord under sewing machine presser foot and bring needle down through cord. Form and stitch loops as you sew, keeping seam of cord always facing up toward you. Continue until all loops are formed and sewn to paper. Pin paper to right side of garment, matching edges. Stitch over the stitching that formed the loops. Tear off paper, apply facing, trim allowances and loop ends to ¼″. Finish opening.

CASINGS

A casing—the special area that holds an elastic or a drawstring—must be wide enough to permit either of them to be pulled freely. It must be equal to the width of the material to be cased plus ⅛″ to ¼″ for its thickness plus ½″ seam allowance.

For an elastic casing, prepare the casing according to pattern instructions, leaving an opening large enough to insert elastic. Insert elastic with a bodkin or safety pin, being careful not to twist it. Lap the ends of the elastic ½″, stitch securely, and finish sewing casing.

For a drawstring casing, you may use either a seam opening or eyelets to pull through the drawstring. If you

177

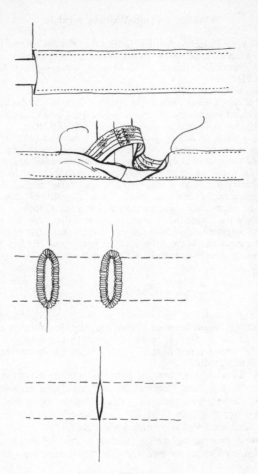

178

are using eyelet openings, prepare them (*see* **BUTTONS,
BUTTONHOLES, AND BUTTON LOOPS**) before the
casing is applied. If you are using a seam opening, leave
the opening wide enough for the drawstring and reinforce
each end of the opening.

COLLARS

The roll, set, and shape of a collar can add much to the
elegance of any fashion, so use the trick that many professional dressmakers use: roll and shape your collar *before* it is sewn to your fashion. And, except in rare cases
such as sheer fabrics, always use an interfacing. It supplies
the necessary crispness and prevents seam allowances from
showing through on the right side of the finished collar.

Collars vary greatly in size and shape, but the rules for
making a perfect collar remain basically the same.

Making a Perfect Collar

- Stay-stitch interfacing, marked side up, to wrong side
  of upper collar. If the collar has corners, trim away
  corners of the interfacing. Now upper collar and interfacing can be handled as one unit.

- Stay-stitch undercollar and pin to upper collar with
  right sides together.

- With interfacing side up, stitch outer edge on marked
  seam line. Do not stitch collar ends yet.

- Trim seam allowances to ¼" and grade them, clipping
  at ¼" intervals.

- Understitch as illustrated. On a collar with corners,
  begin and end understitching 1" from each end.

- A rounded-edge collar is now ready to be turned to

179

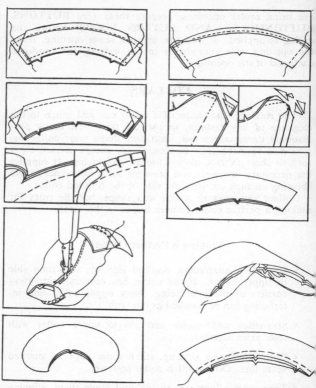

the right side and pressed. A collar with corners is now stitched, on wrong side, across ends.

- Trim corners, press seam ends open with point of iron, trim and grade seam allowances, tapering in toward corners.

180

- Turn collar to right side, pushing out the corners carefully as you turn. Press.

- Now, place collar right side down on a flat surface and roll it back over your hand. Pin the edges together at the neckline. The upper collar seam allowance should be a bit shorter than the lower collar allowance at the neck edge. This is necessary to give the collar a proper roll.

- Stitch the three thicknesses together along the neck seam line exactly as they are placed *after* you have rolled the collar. Do not try to even them before stitching. And your collar is ready to be applied to your garment.

- These directions can be applied to any collar, including one cut as part of the garment body.

Attaching a Collar

A collar can be attached to a garment in a number of ways. It may be attached with a shaped facing that follows the neck edge all the way around, or by a facing across the garment fronts only. Check your pattern to see which method applies to your fashion. And consider the following useful pointers.

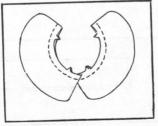

- Always stay-stitch garment neckline so you can safely clip seam allowances before attaching collar.

- If a two-section collar is used, anchor sections together before attaching by overlapping ends at neck seam line and basting across by hand or machine to hold them firmly.

- Sew only the collar to the neckline first. It makes for greater accuracy, and facings can be stitched afterward.

- *See* **FACINGS** for additional information on collar facings.

CORDING

Cording—or tubing—is made by preparing bias strips (*see* **BIAS BINDING**) the desired length and width. Fold strip in half lengthwise, wrong side out. Stitch along length, beginning with a funnel shape *(see diagram)*, and continue stitching, stretching strip as you stitch. Trim seam allowance to a scant ¼" and press seam open with the tip of an iron. Turn tubing with a loop turner or bodkin. Use either instrument or a tapestry needle to pull commercially purchased cable cord through tubing. Cut off excess cable cord. The cording is ready to be used for any number of decorative purposes.

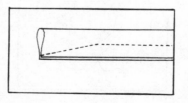

CORNERS
(*see* MITERING)

COUTURE TOUCHES

Couture touches are those elegant extras, usually inside your fashion, which nobody can see but which give you a wonderful, pampered feeling.

Lingerie strap guards prevent shoulder seams from shifting and keep lingeries straps from showing. Cut a 1½″ length of seam binding and sew one end to shoulder seam near armhole. Sew a ball snap to unattached end of seam binding and a socket snap toward neck edge of shoulder seam.

Covered snaps eliminate the unwanted flash of metal and add another touch of elegance to your fashion. Cut a circle of fabric slightly larger than the snap. Place the right side of the snap against the wrong side of the fabric. Make a tiny hole so the ball of the snap goes through, or center the hole over the socket side of the snap. Shirr the edge of the fabric by hand, drawing it over the snap and enclosing it. Fasten the thread securely.

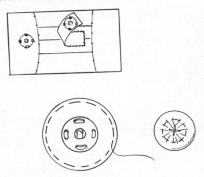

To make hand-made hook eyes *see* THREAD LOOPS.

Inside-waist stays are a must for stretchy fabrics and a true couture touch for any fitted style. Cut a strip of ½"- to 1"-wide grosgrain ribbon long enough to fit waist plus 1" for finishing ends. Turn ends back and stitch. Sew hooks and eyes to ends, extending loops over edge. Tack stay at seams and darts, leaving at least 2" free on either side of zipper.

CUFFS

Cuffs, like collars, come in a wide variety of shapes, styles, and sizes. They may be cut separately and attached to the sleeve, or formed by simply folding back a deep hem. Cuff ends may be closed or open or fastened with buttons or cufflinks.

Cuffs, like collars, should be interfaced for crispness, but it is wise to cut interfacing on the bias for greater resiliency. Remember to cut only half the cuff width for interfacing.

Your pattern sewing guide will tell you how to make and attach your cuffs, but these hints may be valuable.

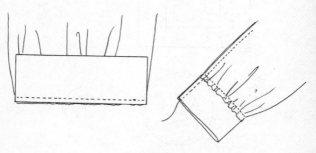

For a cuff with edge seams, follow the instructions for making a perfect collar (*see* **COLLARS**). Just substitute the word *cuff* for *collar*.

To attach a band cuff to a gathered sleeve, it is often easier to attach the cuff *before* you close the sleeve or cuff seams. Stitch the gathered edge of the sleeve to the open cuff, matching all markings. Trim and press seam allowances toward cuff. Then stitch the long underarm seam and cuff seam at the same time.

For a French cuff or a button-link cuff, remember that the inside layer will be on the outside when it is turned back. Therefore, catch-stitch the interfacing to the inside cuff section. Make the two buttonholes that do not show by machine to prevent excess bulk. If you choose, make bound buttonholes in the cuff section that folds up to become the outer part of the cuff (*see* **BUTTONS, BUTTONHOLES, AND BUTTON LOOPS**).

CUTTING THE PATTERN

(See Chapter 6)

DARTS

Darts are the pointed, stitched tucks that shape your fashion to fit your body. To be sure that a dart tapers to nothing, take two stitches at point along fold, as close to fold as possible. And always tie off thread ends to prevent dart points from working open.

Most darts require little additional handling after they are pressed, but deep darts in heavy fabrics should be slashed to within $1/2''$ or so of point and pressed open. Sheers look best when the dart is trimmed. Do this by making a second row of stitching about $1/8''$ from the first. Trim $1/8''$ from this second row of stitching and overcast the raw edges. Contour or double-pointed darts should be clipped at the widest part and then reinforced with a line of stitching parallel to the original dart stitching line.

For dart pressing information, *see chapter 7, page 149.*

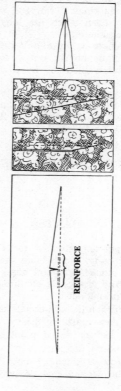

REINFORCE

DECORATIVE TOUCHES

(See **TRIMS***)*

EASING

Easing is the dressmaker's way to accommodate small amounts of fullness caused when one edge is longer than the edge to which it is being joined. Easing is usually indicated by a pair of notches on the pattern set slightly further apart than the notches they are to match—for example, the back edge of a shoulder to the front edge, or the cap of a sleeve to the front and back armhole.

Ideally, easing should be invisible after pressing. It can be if you:

• Always ease the longer edge to the shorter edge. Never stretch the shorter edge to match the longer one.

• Using a slightly longer stitch than normal, make a double row of stitching, rows close together, in the seam allowance between ease notches. The double row will help to insure even distribution of the ease.

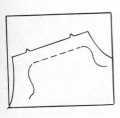 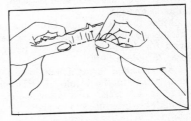

• When you are ready to join sections, pin at notches and at any other markings. Draw up one end of the easing threads until length between notches matches perfectly. With your thumb, gently push fabric along easing threads until it is evenly distributed.

• Stitch with eased edge on top.

• See instructions for pressing sleeves (chapter 7) and use the same techniques for pressing ease.

EQUIPMENT

(See Chapter 5)

FABRICS

(See Chapter 4)

FACINGS

Facings provide a neat finish for raw edges by turning them to the inside of your fashion. They can be separate pieces added to a garment, extensions of cut edges or bias strips. But, whatever type is used, every facing should be smooth and flat.

Most facings are cut from the same fabric as the rest of the garment but a contrasting texture or color may be used for design interest. Or a lighter-weight fabric may be used to reduce bulk.

An extended facing is cut in one piece with the garment and folded to the inside. It is used most often when the edge to be faced is a straight one. An extended facing should be interfaced, especially if a buttonhole closing is planned. Use long running stitches to attach interfacing to garment along the fold line. Catchstitch the remaining edges. Fold back the extended facing along the fold line and press.

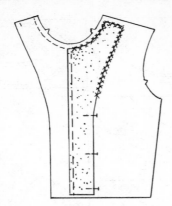

A fitted or shaped facing is cut separately to conform to the shape of the edge being faced—a neckline or armhole, for example. The following step-by-step instructions detail the application of a shaped neckline facing, but they can be used for any shaped-facing application. Follow them carefully for perfect facings every time.

- Join front and back facings. Trim seam allowances to ¼″ and press open.

- Turn under outer edge ¼″ and stitch.

- Trim ⅜″ from outer edge of interfacing.

- Stay-stitch interfacing pieces to wrong side of garment, joining shoulder seams through all thicknesses. Trim all interfacing seam allowances to stitching line. Press open shoulder seams.

- Pin facing to garment with right sides together, matching shoulder seams and notches. Stitch around neck edge.

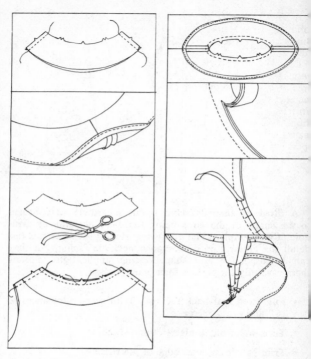

- Trim seam allowances. Then grade and clip seam allowances.

- Understitch facing close to seam line, making sure to catch seam allowance in understitching.

- Turn facing to inside. Catch interfacing to facing. Tack facing to seams to prevent lifting. Press. (*See chapter 7, page 151* for detailed pressing instructions.)

A combination neck-and-armhole facing is applied by following the same method described for a neckline facing. But if your garment has a center back or center front opening, try this quick-and-easy method.

Do *not* sew garment side seams or center seam. Sew *only* shoulder seams of both garment and facing. Trim and press. Apply interfacing as described above. Then stitch facing to neck and armhole edges. Trim seam allowances. Turn by pulling center back or front sections through shoulder openings. After turning, join garment at side seams and continue stitching facing side seams. Press seams open. Stitch center back or front seam.

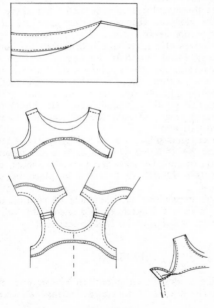

To face with bias facing, prepare bias strip (*see* **BIAS BINDING**). If the bias strip is to be applied to a curve, pre-shape the curve with iron. Baste strip to garment edge, right sides together, beginning at a seam. Stitch bias together at seam where it began. Press seam open. Trim, grade, and clip seam allowances. Turn facing to inside and press. Turn under raw edge, and hem to garment.

FASTENERS

(*See also* **BUTTONS, BUTTONHOLES, AND BUTTON LOOPS** and **ZIPPERS.**)

Snaps are the invisible fasteners used when there is little strain on the closure. **Hooks and eyes** are used at points where there is considerable strain.

The two halves of a snap—the ball and socket—are sewn on separately. Place ball half of snap in position on underside of overlap. Attach by taking 4 or 5 stitches through each hole. Fasten thread securely. Mark location of socket half of snap by pinning opening together and, if there is a hole in ball snap, slip threaded needle (no knot) through ball into socket snap. Attach socket snap the same way you attached ball snap.

To make covered snaps, *see* **COUTURE TOUCHES.**

Hooks can be fastened with straight eyes, when there is an overlap, or round eyes, when two edges meet, or with thread eyes (*see* **THREAD LOOPS**) in place of straight eyes.

Place hook in position on underside of overlap and secure eyelets with 4 a 5 stitches. Slip needle through fabric and take several stitches under ball to secure it.

FITTING

Most fitting is done on the pattern before your fashion is ever cut (*see chapter 2* for proper sizing and *chapter 3*

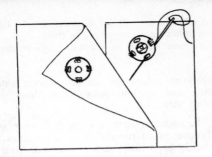

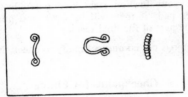

THREAD EYE

STRAIGHT EYE   **ROUND EYE**

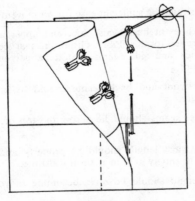

for pattern alterations). What remains should be nothing more than a minor adjustment here or there.

To make those minor adjustments, follow these fitting rules:

- Fit when all seams are stitched, except side seams, waistline, and armhole seams—and these should be pinned or basted.

- Wear the undergarments you plan to wear with your new fashion. And remember to wear shoes with the same height heels that you will wear with your fashion.

- Try on your fashion right side out—always! Pin in shoulder pads if they will be used, and put on belt if it will be part of the final fashion.

- Pin openings closed and get ready to check fit.

Checkpoints for Fitting

- *Do not overfit!*

- There should be sufficient ease for all movements.

- Grain lines at bust, waist, hip, and upper arm should be parallel to the floor. Grain lines at center front and back and side seams should be perpendicular to the floor.

- Center front and back seams should be centered on the figure.

- Shoulder seams should lie across the top of the shoulder.

- Bodice waist length should fit properly and waistline should fit snugly at your natural waistline.

- Skirt length should be most becoming to your figure.

- Sleeve length should be correct, and center elbow dart, if there is one, should point to the tip of the elbow when the arm is bent.

- Bust darts should point directly to the fullest part of the bust.

- Hip darts should point to the fullest part of the hip.

- Sleeve seam line should fit properly around the arm at the shoulder.

- Neckline should fit smoothly.

If any alterations are necessary, mark them and make them. Then, if you wish, re-try on your fashion to confirm a perfect fit.

GATHERING AND SHIRRING

Gathering and shirring are two of the easiest ways to control fullness in a fashion. Both can be done by making a hand running stitch through the section to be gathered. But gathering or shirring by machine is faster, easier, and far more efficient.

To shirr or gather by machine, adjust to the longest stitch and loosen the top tension slightly if the bobbin thread does not pull easily. But for soft, sheer fabrics like chiffon, the gathers will be finer if you use a shorter stitch. Test-stitch first on a scrap to make sure the stitch length is correct.

Distribute fullness evenly by grasping bobbin thread or threads at one end, and gather by easing fabric along threads. At half-way point, fasten threads by winding them around a pin. Repeat the procedure from the opposite end, being careful to distribute fullness evenly.

To press gathers or shirring, *see chapter 7, page 149.*

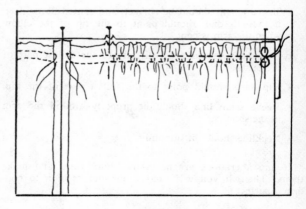

GODETS

Godets are flared or pleated inserts that give added width to the bottom of a skirt while adding a decorative effect. A pie-shaped godet, the most common kind, is usually cut with the straight grain running down the center and the bias edges on each side.

To insert a godet

- Reinforce the garment godet opening by stitching along the seam line where the godet is to be inserted. Stay-stitch the godet, too.

- Slash through the godet opening to the stitched point.

- Pin the godet to the slashed opening, right sides together, matching the seam lines accurately. The seam allowance of the slash will taper to almost nothing at the point.

- Stitch, taking a single stitch across the point. Press seam allowances toward the main part of the garment.

GRADING SEAMS

(*See* **SEAMS AND SEAM FINISHES**)

GUSSETS

A gusset is a small piece of fabric inserted into a slash to provide ease, most often at the underarm of a kimono sleeve. Gusset construction is fairly difficult, but well worth the trouble because it provides a much better fit for a kimono sleeve. Take your time, slash and stitch carefully, reinforce—and you'll turn out a perfect gusset each time.

A **quick-and-easy method** of applying a gusset involves cutting the gusset in half—or two triangles—and inserting each into the sleeve *before* the underarm is stitched. Do it this way:

- Check gusset pattern piece against markings for front and back of bodice. Match markings, and mark gusset pattern piece FRONT and BACK after comparing markings.

- With a ruler, draw a line between the *other* two corners and cut pattern piece in half along the line.

- Pin and cut out each piece of the gusset pattern, allowing an additional ⅝" seam allowance at cut pattern edge. Be sure to continue triangular shape of gusset along sides. *(See diagram)*. Transfer all pattern markings.

- On bodice front and back, reinforce the point of slash *before* cutting. You may reinforce by folding a 3" piece of seam binding into a V and stay-stitching it over the point of the slash. To stay-stitch the point perfectly, stitch to point, pivot needle and take one stitch across point, pivot needle again and stitch to other edge.

- Or you may reinforce the point by stay-stitching, as above, over a small square of iron-on interfacing or firmly woven fabric.

198

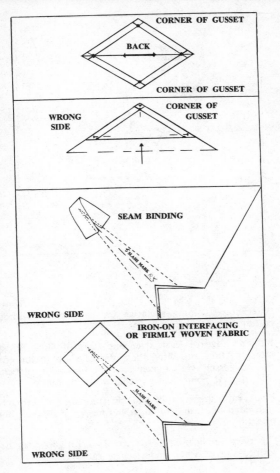

CORNER OF GUSSET

BACK

CORNER OF GUSSET

WRONG SIDE

CORNER OF GUSSET

SEAM BINDING

SLASH MARK

WRONG SIDE

IRON-ON INTERFACING OR FIRMLY WOVEN FABRIC

SLASH MARK

WRONG SIDE

199

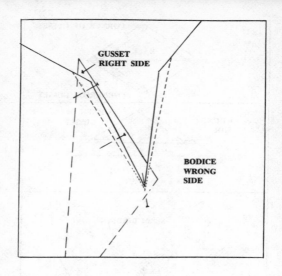

GUSSET
RIGHT SIDE

BODICE
WRONG
SIDE

- After stay-stitching, slash as far as possible without cutting stitch at point.

- Pin one edge of slash over one edge of gusset, right sides together, matching the point of slash to the corner of gusset. Stitch over stitched line with garment side up. At point, leave needle down in fabric.

- Pivot; raise presser foot and pin free edge of gusset to free edge of slash. Stitch as before, over stitched line of slash.

- Complete application of second half of gusset as described above. Stitch underarm seam.

HAND STITCHES

Machine sewing has removed much of the drudgery from clothing construction—but the quality of fashion is still determined by the quality of hand-sewn details.

Use the right needle and thread to suit both fabric and type of stitch (*see* NEEDLE AND THREAD CHART, *chapter 5, page 119*). Use a single 18″ to 24″ length of thread and coat it with beeswax for added strength. Cut thread from the spool at an angle; never break it. And learn to use a thimble; it will make your sewing much easier and more efficient. Keep your stitches loose enough to avoid that puckered look and sew from right to left unless your pattern says otherwise. Left-handers will have to reverse directions.

Running stitch is used primarily for gathering and shirring. Take several small stitches forward and slide stitches onto the thread.

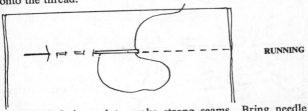

RUNNING

Backstitch is used to make strong seams. Bring needle and thread through fabric on the underside. Take a stitch back, placing it at the beginning of the first stitch and bringing the needle out a stitch ahead. Continue by slipping needle through the end of the last stitch and bringing it out one stitch ahead.

Half-backstitch is also used to make strong seams, to understitch finished facings so they don't roll, and to hand-apply a zipper. Follow the same method for making a backstitch, but carry the needle back only half the length of the last stitch.

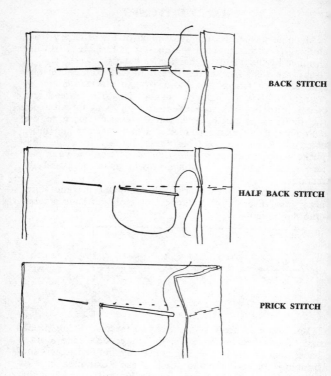

BACK STITCH

HALF BACK STITCH

PRICK STITCH

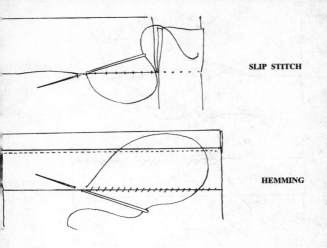

SLIP STITCH

HEMMING

Prickstitch is a variation of backstitch and is often used to apply an elegant hand finish to zippers. Bring needle through fabric from the underside, as for a half-backstitch. Carry the needle back only a few threads and bring needle out again as for a half-backstitch.

Slipstitch is used to hem, attach linings, hold pockets and trims in place, or whenever an almost invisible finish is needed. Slide the needle through the folded edge and pick up one or two threads of the under fabric. Continue this way, taking stitches evenly spaced about ¼" apart.

Hemming stitch is used for all types of hemming and is a bit stronger than slipstitch. Take a tiny stitch in the garment and then bring needle up diagonally through the fold of the hem edge. Space stitches about ¼" apart.

203

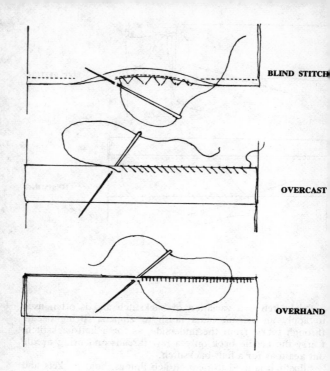

BLIND STITCH

OVERCAST

OVERHAND

Blindstitch is used for hemming, too; but it is virtually invisible on both sides of the garment. First, finish the raw edge to be blindstitched. Then roll this edge back about ¼", take a tiny horizontal stitch through a single thread of the garment, and pick up a thread of the rolled-back edge diagonally above. Be careful not to pull stitches tight.

Overcast stitch is used to finish raw edges. Working from either direction, take diagonal stitches over the raw edge, making them uniform in depth and spacing.

Overhand stitch holds two finished edges together and is usually used to join lace or attach a ribbon to a garment. With right sides together, make small, closely-spaced over-and-over stitches.

Whipstitch is a variation of overhand stitch with the needle inserted at a right angle to the edge, resulting in slanting stitches.

Catch stitch is used to hold two layers of fabric together, most often interfacings to the garment. Working from left to right, take a small stitch through the upper fabric near the edge. Make a stitch through the underfabric from right to left. Continue in this manner so the threads cross each other between stitches.

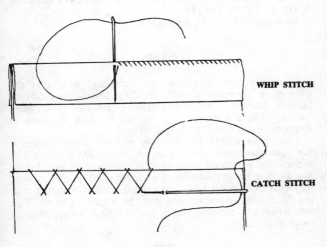

WHIP STITCH

CATCH STITCH

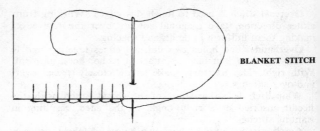

BLANKET STITCH

Blanket stitch is used for a variety of hand-finished details. Work from left to right with the edge of the fabric toward you. Anchor your first stitch at the edge. Then point the needle toward you and insert it through the right side of the fabric about ¼″ above the edge and ¼″ over the last stitch. Keep the thread below your work and *under* the needle.

Buttonhole stitch — *see* **BUTTONS, BUTTONHOLES, AND BUTTON LOOPS.**

Basting stitches—*see* **BASTING**.

HEMS

Hems are both practical—the additional weight at the edge of a garment helps it to hang better—and full of fashion interest. Nothing makes a fashion look more "dated" than a hem that is a bit too short or too long in comparison with the "in" length.

Your hem should be carefully pinned in place after it has been measured. After a try-on, it is quite possible that a perfectly measured hem must be adjusted slightly to allow for the optical illusion often created by plaids, stripes, or pleats. Do make such adjustments even if it means that the final hem measurements may be slightly askew. You are, after all, striving for a visual effect rather than a mechanical one.

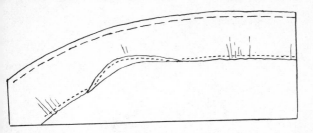

The best hem is the one that is least noticeable. So eliminate bulk, reduce extra fullness, press carefully to prevent ridging *(see chapter 7, page 152)*, and never, never pull your stitches tightly as you hem.

Ease your hem when it has excess fullness. To ease, stitch about ½"from the top of the hem. Matching seams, draw up thread until the hem fits smoothly. Shrink out fullness with your iron *(see chapter 7, page 152)*, finish the raw edge, and sew.

Hem finishes should be determined by both fabric and fashion.

Use **seam binding** for loosely woven fabrics that have a tendency to ravel and for machine-washable fashions. Use woven seam binding for straight hems and bias tape for eased hems. Stitch tape or seam binding over raw edge of the fabric. Hem with a slipstitch. (*See* **HAND STITCHES**).

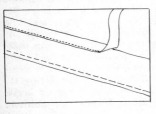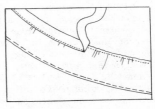

RIGHT SIDE

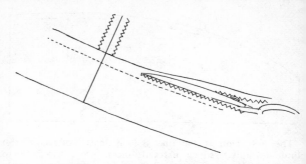

Use a **stitched and overcast** finish on lightweight, firmly woven fabrics. Turn under edge ¼″ and stitch. Baste upper edge of hem to garment and sew with slipstitch, hemming stitch, or blindstitch (*see* **HAND STITCHES**).

Use a **tailor's hem** on bulky or heavy fabrics that won't ravel. Make a row of machine stitching about ¼″ below raw hem edge. Shrink out any excess fullness. Pink edge, and pin or baste hem in place, matching seams. Sew with blindstitch or catchstitch (*see* **HAND STITCHES**).

Use a **faced hem** if the fabric is too bulky for a regular hem, if there is insufficient fabric for a regular hem, or if you want to stiffen a hem with horsehair braid. Ready-made facing is available (*see* **BIAS BINDING**, Bias Fold Tape Chart) or you can make your own bias binding (*see* **BIAS BINDING**). To make a faced hem, mark hemline and trim away excess fabric ½″ outside marking line. Beginning at a seam, place right side of facing to right side of garment, raw edges even. Fold back end, as shown, for a neat finish. Stitch ¼″ from edge. Overlap facing ends. Turn facing to inside along hem marking line and baste close to edge. Press lightly and sew with slipstitch or hemming stitch (*see* **HAND STITCHES**). Slipstitch facing together at joining. To stiffen a hem with horsehair braid, follow the same directions for facing a hem, but substitute braid for facing.

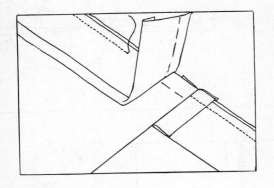

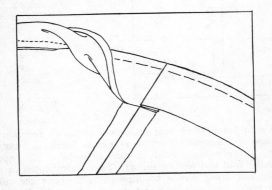

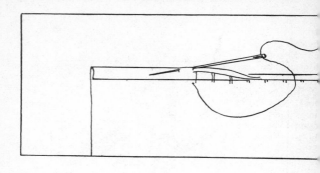

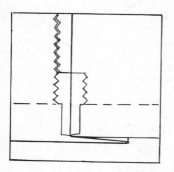

Use a **hand-rolled hem** on sheer fabrics or for scarves, sashes, and lingerie. Trim away excess fabric ¼" outside hem marking line. Fold in raw edge ⅛". Slip needle through fold and anchor thread. Take a tiny stitch in garment and bring needle up through fold above the stitch. Slip needle through fold and repeat. After three or four stitches, draw up thread and a neat, hand-rolled edge is formed.

To **hem with pleats,** follow standard hemming procedure. If a pleat has a seam in it, press seam to one side before hemming. Mark depth of hem on seam above hemline and clip *one* seam allowance at the mark. Press open seam below clip and trim seam allowances to eliminate bulk. Turn up hem and finish.

To **hem a faced opening,** prepare and hem bottom edge first. If the fabric is bulky, trim facing and hem allowance inside of facing to ½", making sure the facing overlap completely covers the trimmed section. Complete hemming bottom edge. Turn facing to inside and baste close to edge. Slipstitch lower folded edges together and secure facing to hem allowance with small catchstitches.

INTERFACING

Interfacing is the crisp reinforcer between the facing and the outer garment that adds body and helps to preserve shape.

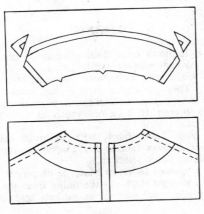

Select your interfacing at the same time you select your fabric so you can make sure they work well together. *See chapter 4, page 96,* for suggested interfacings to use with specific fabric types and weights.

Check your pattern cutting and sewing guides to see where interfacing is needed in your fashion. As a general rule, interfacings are applied to a section before it is stay-stitched or construction-stitched.

To prevent interfacings from adding unwanted bulk to collars, cuffs, and lapels, always trim away corners before attaching, as shown. To prevent bulk at neck zipper openings, trim away ⅝" of interfacing at both sides of neck opening, as shown.

To apply an interfacing under a facing, follow the step-by-step instructions for applying a fitted or shaped facing described in **FACINGS.**

INTERLINING

(See chapter 9, page 300)

LINING

Lining is fashion's inner finish—the shape preserver that is really a garment within a garment.

Linings are a must in tailored garments *(see chapter 9, page 300).* They are also a must in key areas—across the seat of a skirt—if your fashion fabric tends to stretch. And they are a supremely luxurious touch in a dress, blouse, skirt, or slacks.

Choose your lining fabric with as much care as you choose your fashion fabric. *See chapter 4, page 96,* for guides to lining fabric selection.

To line a tailored jacket or coat, *see chapter 9, page 300.*

To line a straight skirt, cut the lining from the skirt pattern, eliminating such details as pockets and waistbands.

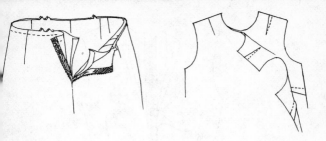

Make the lining separately, following the pattern sewing guide for skirt construction. Before completing the top and placket of the skirt, drop the lining into place with wrong side of lining against wrong side of skirt. Pin the skirt and lining together around the waist. Insert skirt zipper and finish lining at zipper placket by turning under edges and slipstitching (*see* **HAND STITCHES**). Apply the waistband and make each hem separately. The hem on the skirt is turned toward the inside; the lining hem is turned to the inside or construction side.

To line a full skirt, follow the same instructions as for a straight skirt. If, however, the combination of lining fabric and skirt fabric is too bulky at waistline, consider making a straight lining—it can be cut from any straight skirt pattern in the proper size—and attaching it as described above.

To line a shift dress, cut the lining from the shift pattern, cutting 1″ shorter at hem. Sew all darts and seams, and press. Place the lining inside the dress with wrong side of lining against wrong side of dress. Pin lining carefully to dress at neckline and around armholes. Turn under lining edges along zipper, and pin into place. Try on dress with lining to make sure the lining fits smoothly, especially across zippered area. Stitch the lining to the dress within seam allowances at neckline and armholes. Pin neckline and armhole facings in place. Baste and

213

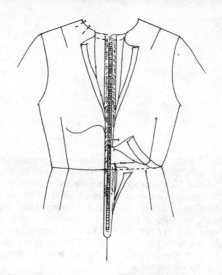

stitch. Trim, clip seams, turn, and press. Finish facings by slipstitching to lining only. Slipstitch lining to the zipper tape. An added row of running stitches (*see* **HAND STITCHES**) along the lining about ¼″ from the edge—catch lining to the zipper tape—will prevent the lining from rolling into the zipper chain and snagging.

To line a dress with a waistline, cut both bodice and skirt linings from pattern. Prepare bodice lining following directions for shift. Prepare skirt lining following directions for skirt. Join bodice and skirt at waistline, making sure to leave bodice and skirt lining free. Apply zipper to garment, leaving lining edges at zipper free. Lap waistline seam allowance of bodice lining over waistline seam allowance of skirt lining and slipstitch. Slipstitch lining zipper edges to zipper tape. Hem skirt and lining separately.

To line a sleeve, *see chapter 9, page 303.*

MACHINE-STITCHING

(See Chapter 5, page 104)

MARKING

(See Chapter 6, page 134)

MITERING

Mitering is the sewer's neat and trim method of eliminating bulk at corners. It is a precise art and takes a bit of practice to execute perfectly, but once you do, you'll add a new dimension to your fashions.

To miter a corner on a pocket, hem, or any applied area requiring a square corner:

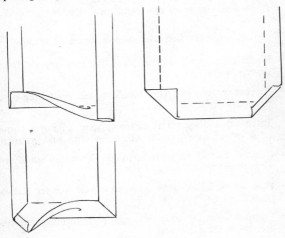

- Turn all seam allowances to the inside and press.

- At the corners, open the seam allowances and turn them to the inside *diagonally* across the point and press.

- Trim corner to ⅜" from the pressed diagonal crease.

- Refold corner along diagonal press line and slipstitch to fasten miter.

OR:

- Follow steps 1 and 2 as above.

- Open out corner and stitch along the pressed diagonal crease.

- Trim the seam, clipping ends so they do not overlap seam allowance press lines.

- Press diagonal seam open and turn to inside. Press.

To miter a top-stitched trim such as braid or ribbon:

- Pin trim in position and hand-stitch or top-stitch the inner edge.

- At corner, fold the trim back on itself, matching outer edges exactly.

- Stitch on a diagonal line, from point of inner corner to point of outer corner, through trim and garment.

- Conceal thread ends inside miter. Trim the small corner formed by stitching, if necessary.

- Pull down folded-back trim and press corner flat on right side.

- Continue pinning trim in position, mitering remaining corners in the same way.

216

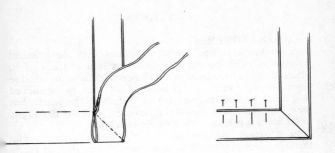

NECKLINES

(*See* **COLLARS**.)

NEEDLES AND THREAD

(*See* Needle and Thread Charts, *chapter 5, pages 119 to 121.*)

NOTIONS

(*See chapter 4. See also* **BIAS BINDING,** Bias Fold Tape Chart.)

PATTERNS

(*See chapter 2* for pattern selection, *chapter 3* for pattern alterations.)

PLACKETS

(See also **ZIPPERS.***)*

A placket is an opening in a garment with the practical purpose of allowing the wearer to get into and out of it. Plackets may be closed with zippers, buttons, or closure tapes—or they may be left open. They may be positioned in a seam or they may be cut as a slash in the fabric, but they must be faced, bound, or hemmed to finish the edges.

To make a placket with a continuous lap:

In a seam: At the bottom of placket opening, clip through seam allowance to seam line. Cut a strip of fabric for lap, either on straight grain or on bias, twice as long as the opening and 1⅞″ wide. Spread out placket opening as shown. Matching edges evenly, pin wrong side of opening edges over right side of strip. Stitch, allowing normal

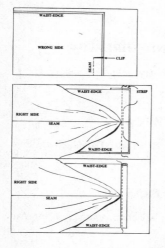

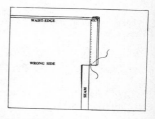

218

eam allowance. To reinforce, double-stitch for about 2″
where seam allowance has been clipped. Trim seam allowance to ¼″. Turn strip away from garment and press.
Make sure seam allowance is also turned away from garment. Turn in free edge of strip ¼″. Press. Fold strip
in half lengthwise, turning it back over seam allowance.
Top-stitch over original row of stitching. Press *(see chapter 7, page 151)*. Turn garment to inside and fold lap at
clipped seam. Stitch diagonally across the fold to secure
it. Fold one side of lap back along seam line and press.

In a slash: Reinforce slash line with stitching *before*
cutting slash. Taper stitching to a point just below slash
line, taking two stitches across point. Slash, but be careful
not to cut into stitches at point. Prepare lap strip as above.
Pin wrong side of first edge of slash over right side of strip,
keeping stitched line on slash ¼″ from edge of lap strip.
Stitch in the direction of the point. At point, leave needle
down in fabric, slip other edge of slash forward and position lap strip under slash edge. Make sure edges are aligned
as for first side. Continue stitching to edge of slash. Trim,
press, and finish as for a seam placket.

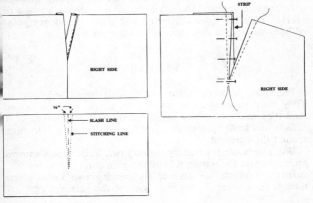

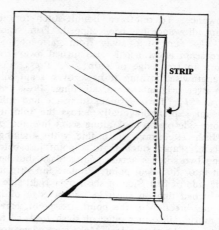

STRIP

To make a faced placket in a slash: Pin facing to garment, right sides together, and follow procedure for reinforcing slash line, except this time you are sewing through garment and facing. Cut slash through both thicknesses of fabric. Turn facing to the inside and press. Reinforce point of opening with a machine- or hand-sewn bar tack.

PLEATS

Pleats are folds in fabric that provide controlled fullness. They may be pressed or unpressed, single or in a series. And they may be formed in any of the following ways:

Side or knife pleats are folded in the same direction around the garment.

Box pleats are formed by turning two knife pleats toward each other on the wrong side of the garment.

Inverted pleats are formed by turning two knife pleats toward each other on the right side of the garment.

220

Accordion pleats are formed by making a series of tiny side or knife pleats around the garment. Accordion pleats are best made commercially.

Understanding pattern markings for pleats: The pattern indicates two lines for each pleat—the *fold line,* along which the fabric is folded, and the *placement line,* along which the folded edge of the pleat is placed. Accurately transferring these markings is extremely important if your pleats are to be uniform.

If you are making your pleats on the right side of the fabric, transfer markings to that side. If you prefer to pleat on the wrong side, you should transfer your markings to that side.

Pressed and unpressed pleats are both made the same way; it is the pressing that makes the difference in appearance.

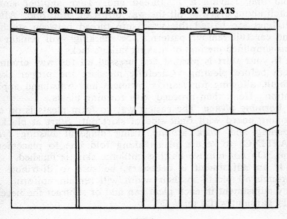

SIDE OR KNIFE PLEATS   **BOX PLEATS**

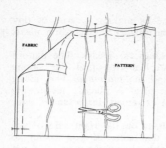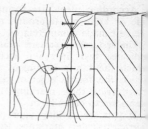

Quick-and-easy marking for a series of pleats: To mark pleats quickly and efficiently, use two thread colors to indicate fold line and placement line. Thread needle with enough thread to reach the entire length of the pleat. Take a small stitch through pattern and fabric at beginning of fold line, leaving a 1″ thread end. Take another small stitch about every 3″ all the way down the fold line. After all lines are basted this way, snip thread between stitches and carefull remove pattern. The markings will remain in this simplified method of making tailor's tacks.

If your skirt is pleated and pressed all the way around hem before pleating. Carefully measure the proper skirt length, allowing for seam allowances and waistband application. Hem; then proceed with forming pleats.

Forming pleats: The easiest way to form pleats is on an ironing board with right side of skirt out. Start at placket opening and work around, using diagonal basting (*see* **BASTING**) to secure pleats along fold line to placement line. Do *not* remove basting until the skirt is finished.

If an adjustment is necessary, be sure to distribute it through all pleats so their width will remain uniform. A tiny adjustment in each pleat can add or subtract the necessary garment width up to 2″.

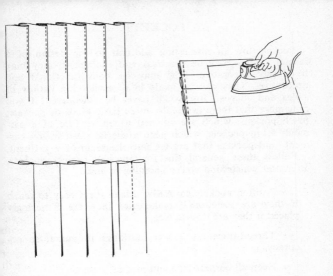

To stitch pleats: Outside stitched-down pleats should be measured from waistline to hipline and marked at each pleat. Top-stitch each pleat from this mark, from hipline up to waistline. Inside stitched-down pleats are similarly marked, but on the inside. Stitch each pleat on inside from this mark, from hipline to waistline. Edge-stitched pleats are top-stitched close to the edge, beginning at the bottom and stitching to the top. Here, too, finish hem before edge-stitching (*see above*). If you wish, you may edge-stitch the lower part of a stitched-down pleat. First, edge-stitch upper fold of pleat from hem to hipline. Then top-stitch from hipline to waistline through all thicknesses of fabric.

To hem a pleat with a seam in it, *see* **HEMS.**

To press pleats, press with steam on *both* sides to establish sharp creases along foldlines both inside and out.

POCKETS

Pockets are an interesting addition to the design of a fashion. They may be practical and functional; they may be purely decorative; they may be both functional and decorative. They can be made in a bewildering variety of styles and shapes. But you'll never be bewildered if you remember that there are really three basic kinds of pockets; patch pockets, which are stitched to the surface of a garment; set-in pockets, which need a special slash in the garment, and pockets that are set into the seam of a garment.

Follow these general tips for precision-perfect pockets, no matter which kind you're planning to make:

- Position pockets carefully. Make them easy to reach if they are functional; make sure they are flatteringly placed if they are decorative.

- Thread-trace all pocket markings to guarantee accuracy.

- Keep all corners true and precise.

- Interface for extra body unless your fabric has a great deal of body by itself.

- Try to make flaps and welts as even and balanced as possible.

To Make a Patch Pocket:

- Turn the raw top edge of the pocket ¼" to the inside and stitch.

- Fold pocket hem to *right* side along fold line. Beginning at fold, stitch along three sides of the pocket along seam line. Do *not* stitch across fold line.

- Fasten thread ends. Trim seam allowance to ⅜", clip

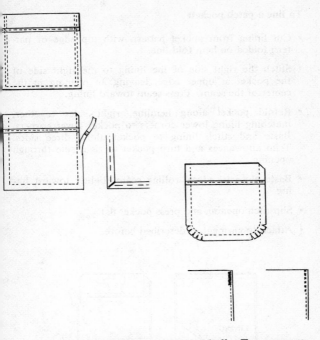

top corners diagonally to eliminate bulk. For a square-corner or pointed pocket, miter remaining corners (*see* **MITERING**). For a rounded pocket, clip through seam allowance at curves.

- Turn to wrong side at stitched line, baste, and press.

- Baste pocket to garment and top-stitch.

- To reinforce top corners, you may make a close zigzag stitch for ¼″ or you may backstitch for ¼″.

225

To line a patch pocket:

- Cut lining from pocket pattern with top edge of pattern folded on hem fold line.

- Stitch the right side of the lining to the right side of the pocket at upper edge, leaving an opening in the center of the seam. Press seam toward lining.

- Refold pocket along hemline, right sides together, matching lining lower corners to pocket lower corners. Baste and stitch lining to pocket along three sides. Trim allowances and turn pocket to right side through opening.

- Baste close to edges, rolling seam slightly toward lining.

- Slipstitch opening and press pocket flat.

- Attach to garment as described before.

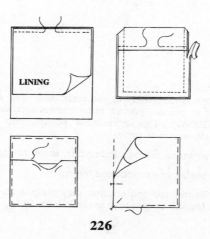

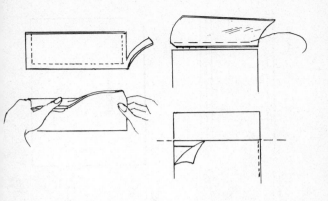

To make a pocket flap.

- Stitch lining to flap, right sides together, leaving upper edge open. Trim allowances and turn to right side.

- Baste close to edges, rolling seam slightly toward lining as you did with lined pocket. Press.

- The flap can be applied in two ways. Pin and baste right side of flap to right side of garment about ¾" above pocket. Stitch in place; fasten thread ends. Trim seam to ¼". Turn flap down and press. From wrong side, sew edges by hand so they do not show. Or, *before* applying pocket, pin and baste flap in place along top marking for patch pocket. Stitch and trim seam allowance. Pin pocket in place, positioning it so that upper edge of pocket is aligned with flap stitch line. Baste and stitch pocket. Remaining seam allowance of flap will be caught in this stitching. Fold flap down over pocket. Press.

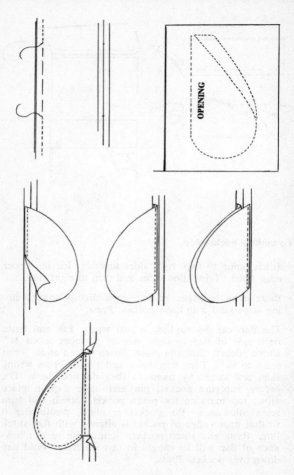

To Make a Seam Pocket:

- This pocket can be set into any side seam or hip seam. Stitch seam, leaving it open between pocket markings. Fasten threads securely at stitching ends.

- Hand- or machine-baste the seam between markings. Press entire seam open.

- Cut pocket of lining fabric according to pattern or make your own pattern *(see diagram)*. The pattern with the straight upper edge is suitable for waistline seams; the pattern with the pointed upper edge is suitable for hipline seams. Make sure the pocket opening is the same as the seam-line opening, plus seam allowances.

- Pin one section of pocket to front seam allowance, right sides together. Stitch ⅜" from edge between markings. Trim seam allowance.

- Press seam open and understitch seam to pocket section. Press pocket section toward front of garment.

- Pin other pocket section to back seam allowance. Stitch ⅜" from edge between markings. Clip back seam allowance to stitching line at top and bottom of pocket. Press pocket section toward front.

- Baste outer edges of pocket together and stitch. Remove basting at seam-line opening.

To Make a Slash Pocket:

- Prepare two strips of fabric—these become the pocket welts—following the same directions as for making **BOUND BUTTONHOLES BY THE TWO-PIECE METHOD.** Continue to follow instruction for apply-

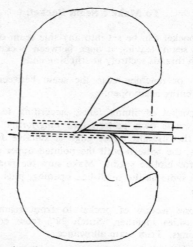

ing a two-piece bound buttonhole, substituting the word *pocket* for *buttonhole*.

- Turn strips to wrong side and catchstitch triangular ends to ends of binding strips as described. Then cut two pocket pieces the same width as the welts. Cut the underpocket section ½" shorter than the upper pocket section.

- Baste and stitch the longer pocket piece along the original stitching line of the upper welt only.

- Place the edge of the under pocket section even with the raw edge of the lower welt. Baste and stitch, sewing through the pocket piece and welt only.

- Turn down lower pocket piece. Match upper and lower pocket pieces at sides and across bottom. Baste and stitch. Press.

PRESSING

(See Chapter 7.)

PREPARING FABRIC FOR CUTTING

(See Chapter 6.)

RUFFLES

The feminine touch of a ruffle—at sleeves or neckline or hem—can add an extra fashion dimension. Make a ruffle if your pattern calls for one, of course. Or add a ruffle if your fashion sense calls for one.

To make a ruffle, cut a strip of fabric on the lengthwise grain to the desired width plus hem and seam allowances. To estimate the length needed, measure the length of the area to which the ruffle will be applied. Double or triple the measured length, depending on the amount of ruffle fullness you want, and cut strip to that length. Hem the lower edge of the strip by machine or by hand. Along upper edge, gather by machine, using a ruffler attachment or using a gathering stitch. *(See* GATHERING AND SHIRRING*).*

To apply a ruffle to an edge, pin ruffle to edge right sides together. Baste if necessary. Stitch with ruffle side up, just beyond the row of gathering stitches. Trim ruffle seam allowance to ¼". Turn under straight edge; then fold it over the raw ruffle edge. Pin and stitch, going over stitching line that attached ruffle to edge. Turn ruffle and press. *(See chapter 7, page 149 for instructions on how to press gathers.)*

To apply a ruffle to a faced edge, pin ruffle, right sides together, to edge to be faced. Baste in place, tapering ruffle at ends. Pin facing over the ruffle and baste. Stitch; trim seam allowances. Turn facing to wrong side, leaving ruffle free. Press.

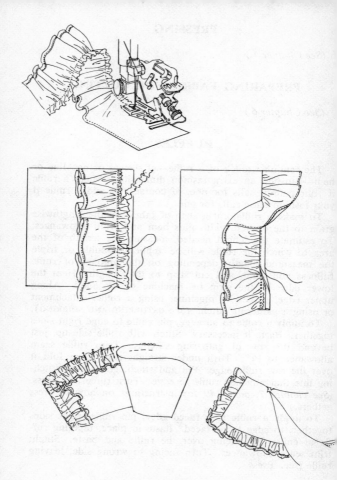

SCALLOPS

The beauty of a scalloped edge is in the perfection of each uniform curve. To get that perfection, follow these suggestions:

• When cutting pattern, do *not* cut out scallops, either on garment or on facing. Instead, cut a straight edge along the top of the scallop cutting line.

• Trace pattern stitching line of scallops on a strip of tissue paper the same length and width as the facing.

• Prepare facing; pin facing to garment edge, right sides together. Pin tissue strip over facing.

• Shorten machine stitch and stitch slowly through tissue along stitching line. Take a single stitch across the base of each scallop before you go on to the next one.

• Remove tissue and cut out scallops, trimming seam allowance to ⅛" to ¼", depending on fabric. Clip into seam allowance around each scallop and toward base of each scallop, being careful not to cut into single base stitch.

• Turn facing to inside and run your fingernail around the inside of each scallop to make sure it turns completely. Press.

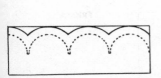 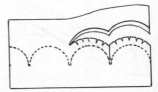

SEAMS AND SEAM FINISHES

Perfect sewing means perfect seams—those lines of stitching that hold a garment together. Perfect seams never pucker or wobble or bulge—and they're finished perfectly with a pinked edge or an overcast edge or a bound edge or a zigzag edge.

Invest some time in studying this section on seams and seam finishes, and your investment will pay off in more professional-looking fashions.

A **plain seam** is made by placing two pieces of fabric together, wrong sides out and edges even, and stitching along seam line.

A **French seam** is made by placing two pieces of fabric together, right sides out and edges even, and stitching ⅜" from the seam line *in* the seam allowance. Trim the seam to within ¼". Turn and press. With wrong sides out, stitch along seam line, encasing raw edge. (*See chapter 7, page 147, for pressing instructions.*)

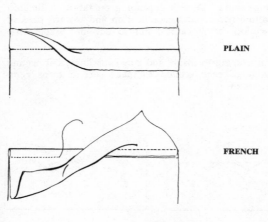

PLAIN

FRENCH

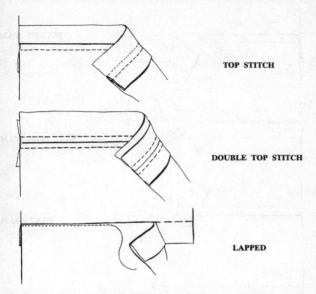

TOP STITCH

DOUBLE TOP STITCH

LAPPED

A **top-stitched seam** is made by pressing a plain seam to one side and top-stitching the desired distance from seam on the right side of the garment through all thicknesses of fabric.

A **double top-stitched seam** is made by pressing open a plain seam and top-stitching the desired distance from each side of the seam on the right side of the garment through all thicknesses of fabric.

A **lapped seam** is made as follows: one section is lapped over the other and top-stitched. Fold under the seam allowance on the section to be lapped and press flat. Working from the right side, pin folded edge over the remaining section with the fold along the seam line. Stitch close to the fold through all thicknesses of fabric.

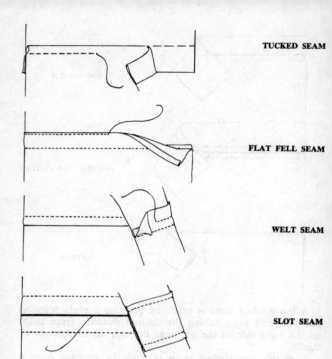

TUCKED SEAM

FLAT FELL SEAM

WELT SEAM

SLOT SEAM

A **tucked seam** is made as follows: prepare as for a lapped seam and slip-baste the fold in place. To form the tuck, stitch through all thicknesses at the desired depth. Remove basting.

A **flat-fell seam** is made as follows: place sections wrong sides together and stitch a plain seam. Press the seam to one side and trim lower seam allowance to ⅛". Turn under the edge of the other seam allowance ¼" and place

236

over trimmed seam allowance. Stitch close to the folded edge through all thicknesses of fabric.

A **welt seam** is made as follows: place sections right sides together and stitch a plain seam. Trim the lower seam allowance to ¼". Stitch through the upper seam allowance and garment close to the trimmed edge, encasing the lower seam allowance.

A **slot seam** is made as follows: with right sides together, machine- or hand-baste a plain seam. Press open. Cut a strip of fabric as long as the seam and slightly wider than both seam allowances. With strip below work, top-stitch the same distance on each side of the seam on right side. Remove basting.

A **piped seam** is made as follows: baste piping to the right side of one fabric section along the seam line. Place the second section over the piping, right sides together, and baste. Stitch on seam line through all thicknesses of fabric.

A **corded seam** is made as follows: encase cording (*see* **CORDING**). Follow directions for making a piped seam,

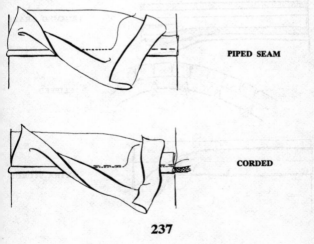

PIPED SEAM

CORDED

using cording instead. Stitch through all thicknesses of fabric, using a cording or zipper foot.

Once your seams have been stitched, they need to be trimmed and finished. To **trim** a seam allowance, simply cut excess to ¼″ or ⅜″. To eliminate bulk when more than two thicknesses of fabric have been stitched together, **grade** seam allowances by cutting each allowance to a different width. Begin by trimming interfacing, if used, closest to stitching line; then trim next layer of fabric a little further away from stitching line, and so on.

Curved seams should be **clipped** to permit the seam to lie flat. Corners should be tapered to eliminate bulk. Inside corners should be clipped for the same reason.

Extra-sturdy seams or **seams in stretchy fabrics** should be taped. Place a strip of woven seam binding along the stitching line. Stitch through tape as you stitch the seam.

The kind of **seam finish** you choose will depend in great part on the fabric you are using. But *do* finish all raw edges to prevent raveling, to insure durability, to help the

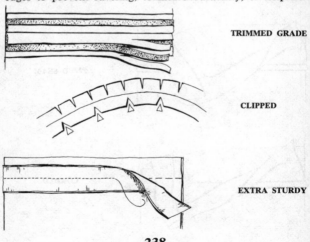

TRIMMED GRADE

CLIPPED

EXTRA STURDY

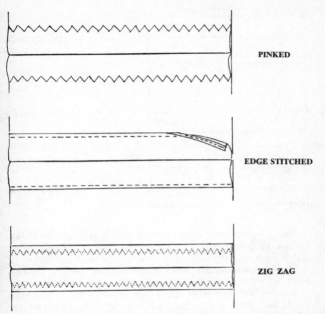

PINKED

EDGE STITCHED

ZIG ZAG

seam allowances support the garment shape—and to give the same neat finish to the inside of your fashion that you strive for on the outside.

Use a **pinked** or **scalloped finish** if your fabric is firmly woven and will not ravel. Use pinking or scalloping shears and cut along raw edges with long, even strokes.

Use an **edge-stitched finish** if your fabric has a tendency to ravel slightly. Machine-stitch ⅛″ from the raw edge.

Use a **zigzag finish** if your fabric ravels and needs a secure finish. Zigzag by machine close to the raw edge. Use a smaller stitch on firmly woven fabrics, a wider stitch on loosely woven fabrics.

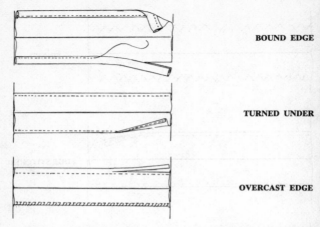

BOUND EDGE

TURNED UNDER

OVERCAST EDGE

Use a **bound edge finish** if your fabric is heavy or bulky. Encase each raw edge in commercial double-fold bias tape. Stitch with slightly narrower edge of the tape on top.

Use a **turned-under edge finish** for lightweight fabrics. Fold under raw edges ¼″ and stitch ⅛″ from the edge.

Use an **overcast edge finish** for most fabrics. Machine-stitch ¼″ from raw edge and trim to ⅛″. Overcast the edge by hand (*see* **HAND STITCHES**), using the machine stitching as a guide.

SEWING MACHINE AND ATTACHMENTS

(See Chapter 5.)

SEWING TOOLS

(See Chapter 5.)

SLEEVES

Nothing sets off a garment better than a well-made, properly fitted sleeve—and nothing stamps a fashion as being "home-made" quicker than a poorly made sleeve. Perhaps this is why many sewers feel a twinge of anxiety when they begin to construct a sleeve.

Put your anxiety to rest—and make a perfect sleeve every time—by remembering these basic rules.

- Always transfer *accurately* all sleeve and armhole markings from pattern to fabric.

- Always make sure your shoulder fitting is correct. Even the most expert sleeve application will be distorted by a poorly fitted shoulder seam.

SET IN

RAGLAN

KIMONO

- Pressing is an essential step in properly shaping the sleeve *(see chapter 7)*.

- Pinning and basting a sleeve are musts that cannot be omitted.

Sleeve styles may range from the casual to the ultra-sophisticated, but most of them fall into three basic types. The first is the *set-in sleeve,* which is joined to the garment by a seam that encircles the armhole. The second is the *raglan sleeve,* which is joined to the bodice by a diagonal seam extending to the neckline. The third is the *kimono sleeve,* which is cut in one with the bodice.

The Set-in Sleeve

- To guarantee perfect application, run a single line of thread tracing along the crosswise grain of the sleeve cap just above the notches.

- Make a row of ease-stitching—set your machine to 10 stitches to the inch—along seam line of the sleeve cap between notches. A second line of ease-stitching, about ⅛" above the first and in the seam allowance, will help to control cap fullness uniformly.

- If the sleeve is long or three-quarter length, easing or darts will be needed to shape the elbow. Follow pattern instructions, or check DARTS and EASING.

- Stitch underarm seam. Press open.

- Complete the sleeve finish at hem according to pattern instructions. See **CUFFS** if a cuff application is necessary.

- With garment wrong side out, place sleeve in the armhole, right sides together. Pin together at underarm seams, notches, dots, shoulder seam.

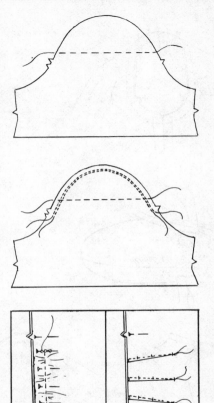

LONG OR ¼ SLEEVE

243

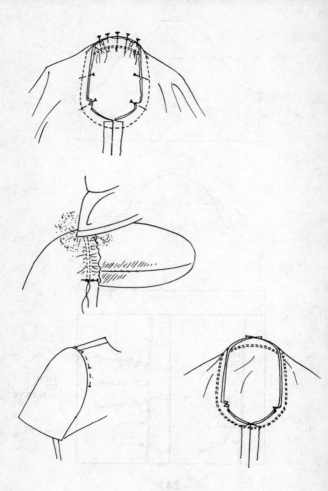

• Gently gather up easing threads until the sleeve fits the armhole. Secure easing threads around a pin.

• Distribute fullness carefully, leaving 1" of flat area at the shoulder seam where the grain of fabric does not permit easing. As you ease fullness, be sure *not* to pull markings and seam line out of alignment.

• With easing threads fastened *securely* around pin, remove sleeve from armhole. Press sleeve cap, following instructions in *chapter 7 (page 150)*.

• Pin sleeve back into armhole as before, adding pins at 1" intervals all the way around. Baste.

• To double-check sleeve before stitching, turn garment to right side and turn seam allowance toward the cap of the sleeve. You should have a smooth cap without puckers or dimples.

• When cap is satisfactory, turn garment back to inside and, starting at underarm seam, stitch around armhole. Make a second row of stitching within seam allowance ¼" from first row.

• Trim armhole seam close to second row of stitching and zigzag or overcast the remaining seam allowance.

• Turn seam allowance toward sleeve cap, but *do not* press.

The Raglan Sleeve

• Stitch the shoulder dart of the sleeve, slash toward point, and press open. See **DARTS** and dart pressing information in *chapter 7 (page 149)*.

• Join the sleeve to the front and back bodice sections, right sides together, carefully matching notches and edges. Stitch and clip seams at intervals. Press.

245

• Pin the underarm seam of bodice and sleeve and stitch them in one continuous seam. Press. If necessary, clip at the underarm seam to make it lie flat and smooth.

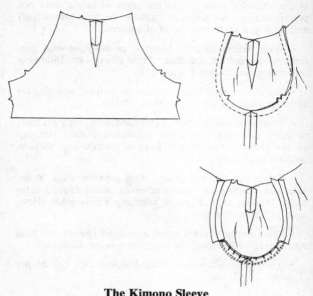

The Kimono Sleeve

• An ideal choice for beginning sewers, the kimono sleeve is the easiest to make. With right sides together, join bodice front and back at shoulder. Stitch. Press according to instructions for pressing curved seams, *chapter 7 (page 147)*.

• Join bodice front and back, with right sides together, at underarm, and baste.

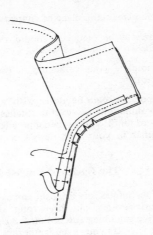

• Place a strip of straight seam binding over the basting line. Stitch the seam through the seam binding. Slash seam allowances at the underarm curve, being careful not to slash seam binding. Press.

For a kimono sleeve with a gusset, follow the quick-and-easy method for applying a gusset outlined under GUSSETS. After the gusset is applied, stitch underarm seam and press.

SMOCKING

Smocking is the fine art of holding fabric together in even, decorative folds. If your pattern calls for smocking, a transfer sheet with guide dots will be supplied, along with instructions for use. Or, if your prefer, you can add a touch of smocking to your fashion, keeping the following points in mind:

247

- Keep smocking clear of shaped edges such as armholes

- Area to be smocked should measure three times the finished or smocked width.

- Complete your smocking before assembling your garment.

- Smocking can be done with a variety of stitches or combinations of several stitches. Learn them; practice them until you've become adept; then put them together in your own design or with a transfer pattern

The Basics of English Smocking

The technique of English smocking involves gathering the fabric evenly on the wrong side first, then making decorative smocking stitches on the right side.

Begin by drawing even gathering stitches on the wrong side. Use strong thread with a secure knot. Gather across each row and leave thread end hanging. When all rows are gathered, pull all threads to form even pleats. Secure hanging threads by knotting them together, two by two, as shown.

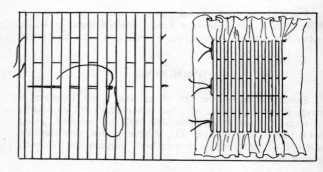

248

On the right side, use six-strand embroidery floss to make the decorative stitches of your choice. To begin a row, bring needle out in first pleat with right side of fabric facing you. Take two tiny backstitches over the pleat fold to secure thread. To finish a row, bring needle to wrong side through fold of last pleat. Take two tiny backstitches in place and cut thread.

To make a honeycomb stitch:

• With thread above needle, put needle through first pleat, about ¼" below tacking stitches. With thread

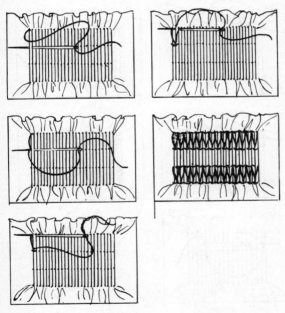

below needle, put needle through second pleat at same level. Pull thread tightly together. Bring needle up to first level. With thread above needle, put needle through third pleat. Pull thread tightly together. Repeat to end of row, and repeat row as desired.

To make a trellis stitch:

- With thread above needle, put needle through second pleat. Slant needle down slightly. Put needle through third pleat the same way. With thread below needle,

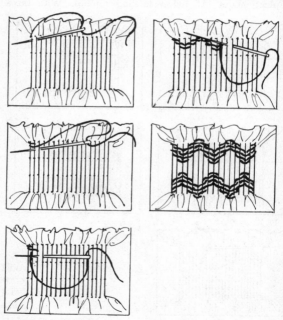

put needle through fourth pleat horizontally. Put needle through fifth and sixth pleats, slanting needle up slightly. With thread above needle, put needle through seventh pleat horizontally. Repeat to end of row, and repeat row as desired.

STAY-STITCHING

(See Chapter 6, page 137.)

TACKING

Tacks are special thread reinforcements that help keep pockets and pleats and seams from ripping while adding a decorative touch. They are most often made by hand with buttonhole twist or embroidery floss.

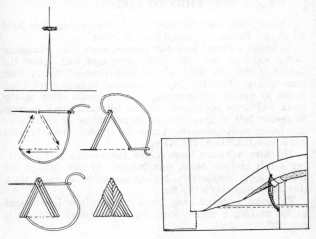

251

A **bar tack** is made by taking several long stitches across the end of an opening. These long stitches are covered by a series of overhand stitches taken across them.

An **arrowhead tack** is made as follows: Mark a small, triangular outline on the right side of the fabric. Begin by bringing needle out at lower left-hand corner and taking a small stitch across upper corner from right to left. Bring needle down into lower right-hand corner and pull it out at left corner next to first stitch. Continue working around triangle until the entire area is filled in.

A **French tack** is made *inside* a garment to hold two parts, usually a lining and outer shell, loosely together. Draw needle through first garment section and into second section, holding the two sections apart the desired amount. Make three or four additional stitches between two parts, keeping desired separation, and secure thread. Cover the stitches with a blanket stitch (*see* **HAND STITCHES**).

THREAD LOOPS

Thread loops are the nearly invisible carriers that hold a belt or a button or a metal hook in place.

To make a thread loop belt carrier, mark loop placement —the width of the belt—half above and half below the center of the belt line. Use a long, doubled thread with ends securely knotted. Insert needle at bottom mark from inside to outside of garment. Take a small stitch at top mark and draw up thread, leaving sufficient slack in loop to permit belt to move freely. Repeat three or four times and fasten thread securely. Cover the stitches with a blanket stitch (*see* **HAND STITCHES**).

To make a button loop, follow instructions as for making a belt carrier. Make sure button will slip through the finished loop comfortably, but do not allow so much slack that the button might slip free.

To make a thread loop for a hook, follow instructions as for making a button loop, but draw thread so there is practically no slack.

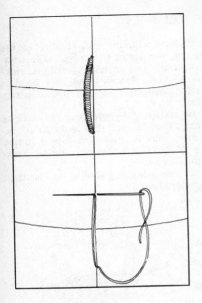

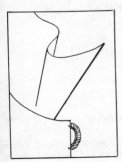

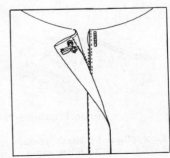

TRIMMING

Nothing stamps a fashion with the individuality of the sewer so much as the creative use of trimmings. The trimming counters are full of the raw materials—fringes, rickracks, braiding, beads, sequins, ribbons—and your head is full of creative ideas for their use. So it is just a matter of putting them together.

Don't let yourself be restricted by preconceived notions of what goes with what. The rickrack that looks so adorable on a little girl's dress may be marvelous—in a jumbo size—on her mother's skirt. Or a fringe may be an unexpected bonus on a tailored dress.

But always remember that trimming should do just that; trim a fashion and not overwhelm it.

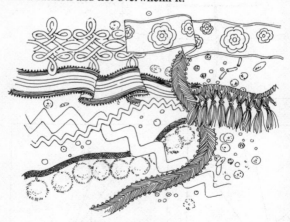

Some Trimming "How-To's"

To appliqué by hand: Transfer design to appliqué fabric and stitch close to outer edges. Trim to ⅛″ beyond stitchng line. Baste in position. Attach with a small blanket stitch (*see* **HAND STITCHES**) or turn under raw edges to stitching line and attach with invisible slipstitches (*see* **HAND STITCHES**). **By machine:** Cut appliqué with a 1″ seam allowance. Back with a lightweight but stiff backing —organdy works well—and baste both to garment. Stitch with a close zigzag stitch. Trim away excess fabric. If you are overlapping several appliqués, do *not* stitch those portions that will be covered.

To apply beading: Using a fine needle and thread waxed with beeswax (*see* Needle and Thread Chart, *chapter 5, page 119*), sew on single beads with a backstitch. Sew on a string of beads by taking a stitch over the thread between each bead.

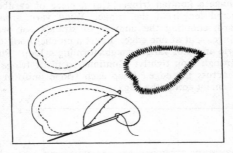

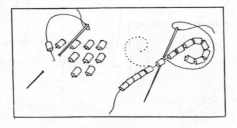

To make a tailored bow: You will need a length of rib bon or bias strip (*see* **BIAS BINDING**) three times the de sired length of the bow. Fold the fabric in half and stitch across width slightly less than halfway from ends. Bring stitching line to center fold and tack securely. Wrap smaller strip of ribbon or bias around the bow at the center to create the illusion of a knot. On the underside, lap on end of the smaller strip over the other and whipstitch (*see* **HAND STITCHES**) to secure.

To make a self fringe: Make sure the edge to be fringe is cut on a single thread of the straight grain of the fabric Mark the depth of the fringe and stay-stitch along this line Working from the edge in, gently ravel the threads of th fabric to the line of stay-stitching.

To make a knotted fringe: Cut a piece of cardboard to the desired length of the fringe. Wind yarn around the cardboard, counting the number of strands you want for each fringe. Cut at one edge. Insert a crochet hook through the fabric and pull yarn through, forming a loop. Pull yarn ends through loop tightly. Continue to place fringe as de scribed across the edge. Keep each fringe uniform in size and placement across the edge.

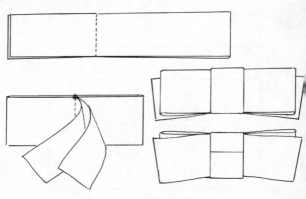

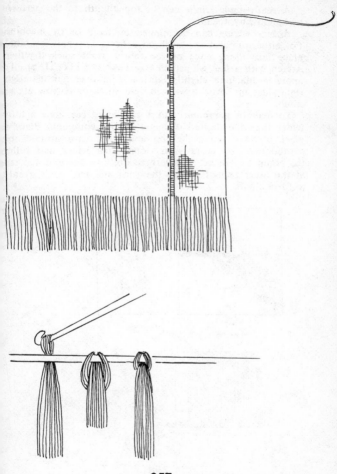

257

A ready-made fringe can be top-stitched to the garment by hand or by machine.

A lace edging can be applied by hand or by machine. For either application, finish edge first. To apply by hand, place lace along edge of the fabric, right sides together. Attach with a fine whipstitch (*see* **HAND STITCHES**). To apply by machine, slightly lap lace edge over finished edge, right sides up. Attach with straight stitch or narrow zigzag stitch.

To make a pompom: Cut a cardboard rectangle a little wider than the desired diameter of the pompom. Place a piece of yarn along the top and wind yarn around the cardboard. The more yarn wound, the wider and fuller the pompom will be. Tie yarn securely at one end and cut at the other end. Fluff up the yarn and trim ends evenly to form a ball.

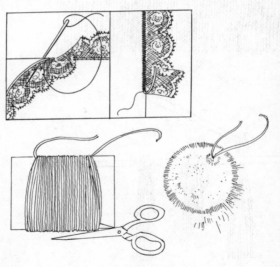

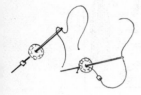

To apply sequins: Use a fine needle and thread waxed with beeswax (*see* Needle and Thread Chart, *chapter 5, page 119*). To apply sequins singly, bring needle from wrong side up through fabric and center of sequin. Slip a tiny bead over the needle and bring needle back down through center of sequin. Fasten thread or continue to apply sequins. *To apply a row of sequins,* bring needle through fabric and center of sequin. Take a backstitch in the fabric and draw up thread until sequin is flat. Apply the next sequin in the same way, keeping sequin edges overlapped.

To apply rickrack: A strip of rickrack can be applied by hand or by machine. To apply by hand, bring needle up through fabric and point of rickrack. Bring needle back through fabric close to rickrack point and diagonally up through next point. To apply by machine, stitch through center of rickrack.

To apply any ribbon, braid, or binding with a mitered corner, see instructions for **MITERING.**

To make a tassel: Follow the instructions for making a pompom, but wind less than half the amount of yarn around the cardboard, depending on the fullness you desire for each tassel. After fastening yarn on top and cutting yarn at the bottom, wind another piece of yarn as shown. Tie securely and trim ends.

TUCKS

A tuck is a slender fold of fabric that can be a construction feature or a decorative feature—or both.

Dart tucks (*see* **DARTS**) are most often stitched on the wrong side of the garment. They control fullness and shape much as regular darts do—but dart tucks do not come to a tapered point. Instead, they release fullness at one or both ends.

Pin tucks are delicate, narrow tucks spaced evenly apart and stitched on the right side of the garment.

Blind tucks touch or overlap each other, and *spaced tucks* are formed at a regular, predetermined space from each other.

But all tucks, no matter what their style or type, should be precision-made and uniform.

260

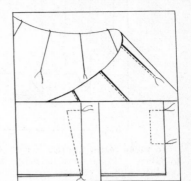

DART TUCKS

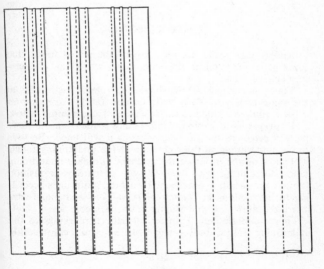

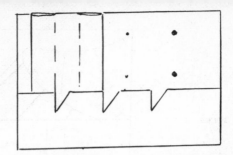

To make tucks, transfer markings carefully from pattern to fabric. Use a ruler or gauge to keep tuck depth and spacing uniform. Follow pattern sewing guide for stitching instructions. For pressing instructions, *see chapter 7, page 149*.

UNDERLINING

Underlining is the fashion shaper—the added touch that gives a garment longer life, cuts down wrinkling, and creates beautiful body.

Your underlining fabric should be selected carefully at the same time you select your fashion fabric. *See chapter 4* for a complete guide to the selection of underlining fabric.

To prepare underlining: Underlining is cut from the same pattern pieces as the garment sections it will back. Be sure to cut underlining so the right side of the underlining fabric will show on the inside of the garment. Prepare underlining fabric for cutting the same way you prepare your fashion fabric—preshrink, if necessary, straighten grain lines according to instructions in *chapter 6, page 124*—and make sure that both fabric and underlining grain lines coincide.

To cut underlining: Transfer all pattern markings to the underlining fabric only—they will be your construction

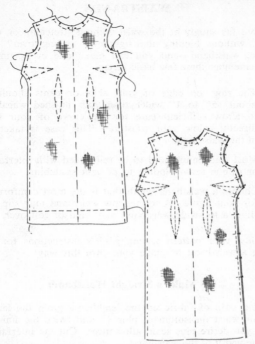

guides, since underlining and outer fabric sections will be stitched together.

To sew underlining: Pin and baste each underlining section to its fabric counterpart, matching notches and checking that grain lines match. Machine-baste through the centers of darts, tucks, or pleats to eliminate shifting of the two layers during construction. Continue garment construction according to your pattern sewing guide, treating the two layers as one fabric.

WAISTBANDS

What fits snugly at the waist without stretching or wrinkling, without binding too tightly or rolling over? The perfect waistband—and you can make one every time if you remember these few basic facts:

- The raw top edge of your skirt or pants should be about ½″ to 1″ wider than your finished waistband to allow sufficient ease for the curve of your body directly below your waistline. This ease is taken up in the waistband.

- Most waistbands need to be reinforced with interfacing or ribbon seam binding to prevent stretching.

- Choose a waistband width that is the most comfortable for your figure. A too-narrow waistband may slip and slide; a too-wide waistband may bind or roll over.

Follow your pattern sewing guide's instructions for applying a waistband or make your own this way:

To Make a Straight Waistband:

Cut a strip of fabric on the lengthwise grain the length of your waist measurement plus 3″ and twice the finished width you desire plus seam allowances. Cut the interfacing half the width of the waistband.

To Apply a Straight Waistband:

- Attach the interfacing to the inside of the half of the waistband that will be stitched to the skirt or pants by basting along the fold line—for later top-stitching—or slipstitching (*see* **HAND STITCHES**) for an invisible finish.

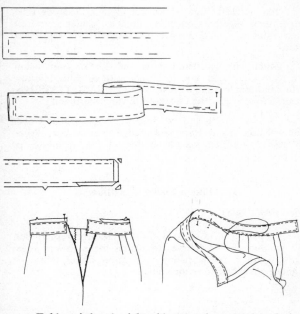

• Fold waistband, right sides together and interfacing attached, and pin across ends and back extension edge.

• Stitch across ends and to back extension mark. Clip diagonally at mark to end of stitch line and trim seam allowances.

• Turn and press carefully, using a point presser to get into the corners.

• Turn under edge of waistband without interfacing along the seam line and baste. Turn entire waistband to right side and press.

265

• Pin notched edge of waistband to outside of skirt, right sides together, matching notches, center markings, and front edges. Ease skirt as necessary to waistband. Baste.

• Stitch with waistband above and skirt or pants below on seam line. Trim interfacing close to stitching line and trim and grade (*see* **SEAMS AND SEAM FINISHES**) seam allowances. Press seam up toward waistband.

• Turn to inside and lap free edge of waistband over the waistline seam. Hem folded edge to seam line. Press. If desired, topstitch waistband through all thicknesses of fabric.

To Make a Faced Waistline:

(*See* **FACINGS**)

• Prepare a strip of ¾"- to 1"-wide grosgrain ribbon by steaming it into curves to match the waistline edge. Or prepare a fabric facing strip from lining fabric or lightweight fabric to reduce bulk.

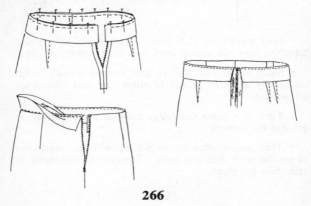

• Pin the facing or ribbon strip to the waistline, easing to fit, with right sides together. Stitch, trim, and grade seams.

• Understitch facing close to seam line to prevent rolling to the outside (*see* **FACINGS,** illustration).

• Turn and press. Turn under ends and sew securely to zipper tape. Tack facing or ribbon strip to garment at seams and darts. Sew hook-and-eye closing to facing at top of zipper on the inside.

For inside waist stays, *see* **COUTURE TOUCHES.**

ZIPPERS

Big and brassy and pointedly decorative, or flexible and almost invisible, the zipper is the busy sewer's convenient closing.

Although the very sound of the word can scare the beginning sewer, a zipper application is easy enough if the zipper has been properly selected according to weight and style—and if you remember these helpful hints.

• Close the zipper and press out all creases before applying. But press carefully with a press cloth and a dry iron. If the iron temperature is too high or the zipper teeth are not protected, the zipper may no longer slide with ease.

• Preshrink the zipper if it will be applied in a washable garment.

• Always use a zipper foot when you machine-stitch a zipper.

• Whether you stitch by hand or by machine, learn to use the sewing guideline that is woven into many zipper tapes.

• Always sew both sides of your zipper in the same direction.

• To stitch past the zipper slider, leave the needle in the fabric, raise the zipper foot and move the slider either up or down to get it out of the way.

• And this hint for zipper maintenance: if your zipper seems stiff and hard to operate after laundering, run a piece of beeswax or soap over the coils.

Selecting the Right Zipper

A *skirt zipper* opens at the top, is usually lightweight, and ranges in length from 6″ to 9″.

A *neckline zipper* opens at the top, is usually lightweight, and ranges in length from 4″ to 36″. It may be used for

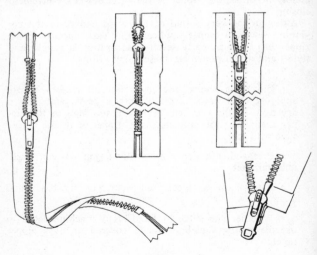

necklines, sleeve openings, and underarm blouse plackets, among other applications.

A *dress zipper* is closed at both top and bottom, is usually lightweight, and ranges in length from 10″ to 14″. For comfort's sake, choose the longer lengths for closely-fitting dresses.

A *trouser zipper* opens at the top, is of heavier weight than dress, skirt, and neckline zippers, and is available in an 11″ length, which may be cut as necessary.

A *separating* or *jacket zipper* opens at both ends and is available in light weights in lengths from 10″ to 24″ and in heavy weights in lengths from 14″ to 24″.

There are two basic zipper applications: the *centered* zipper, where the two edges of the opening meet over the center of the zipper, and the *lapped* zipper, where one edge of the opening forms a lap that completely conceals the zipper *and* the line of stitching on the other edge.

To Prepare for Any Zipper Application:

• Change from regular presser foot to a zipper foot.

• Make sure the length of the garment opening is adjusted to accommodate the zipper. On a skirt placket, allow the length of the zipper with tab turned up plus the waist seam allowance. On a dress placket, allow the length of the zipper with the tab turned up. On a neck placket, allow the length of the zipper plus an additional ½″ to accommodate a hook-and-eye. If the neckline is unfinished at the time the zipper is applied, allow the neckline seam allowance, too.

To Apply a Centered Zipper:

- Machine-baste zipper opening together on seam line. Press basted seam open.

- Turn garment to inside. Place zipper, tape down and tab pulled down to bottom, along right-hand *single* seam allowance. Make sure bottom of zipper is at bottom of basted opening and zipper teeth are against basted seam line. Hand- or machine-baste along zipper sewing guideline. (If application is being made to an unfaced neckline or skirt edge, trim off excess zipper tape above seam line and continue stitching to end.)

- Close zipper. (Trim off excess zipper tape on opposite side if necessary.) Turn garment away from remaining seam allowance and hand- or machine-baste remaining zipper tape to other *single* seam allowance along zipper sewing guideline.

- Turn garment to right side and adjust machine stitch for regular stitching. Starting at top of zipper placket, stitch down along one side of zipper to end. Raise zipper foot, keeping needle in work, and pivot garment. Stitch across bottom of zipper. For uniformity, count the cross stitches taken to basted seam and make the same number of stitches to seam line on other side of the zipper. Pivot again and stitch other side of zipper to top of placket.

- Remove original basting along seam line and press, following instructions for pressing plackets in *chapter 7 (page 151)*.

- For an elegant hand-finished look, use a hand prick-stitch (*see* **HAND STITCHES**) instead of machine-stitching on top side of placket.

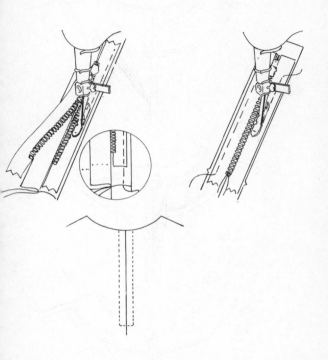

*To finish a neckline or skirt facing after the zipper has
been applied,* press facing down over zipper tape. Turn
under raw edges of facing and slipstitch over zipper tape,
slanting away slightly at lower edge. Sew a hook and
eye on inside above zipper.

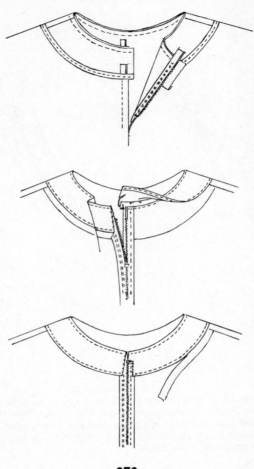

To Apply a Lapped Zipper in a Skirt:

- Machine-baste zipper opening together on seam line. The seam allowances should be at least ⅝″ wide to allow for proper lapping. If allowance is too narrow, widen it by stitching a length of seam binding over the raw edge of the allowance that will form the lap. Press basted seam open.

- Turn garment to inside. Place zipper tape down with tab up at edge of garment along right-hand *single* seam allowance. Make sure zipper is positioned so that its teeth or coils lie *fully* on the extended seam allowance just touching the basting line. Stitch along zipper tape sewing guide, checking positioning every inch or so.

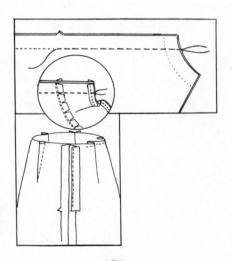

273

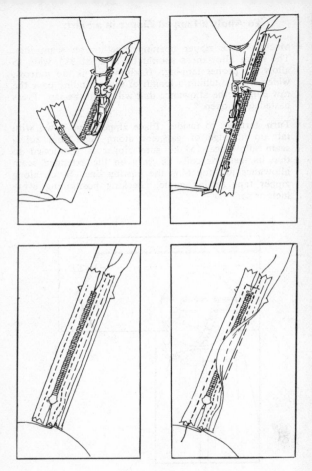

- Turn seam allowance under and zipper face up—this is a single turning operation—and a fold forms in seam allowance. Bring fold close to coil or chain—but not close enough to touch—and adjust to regular stitching. Top-stitch fold to zipper tape the full length of the tape.

- Spread garment flat on wrong side and turn zipper face down again over free seam allowance. As you do so, a pleat will form at each end of the top-stitched part of the placket. Stitch across zipper tape and pleat at bottom of zipper through all thicknesses, stopping at zipper tape sewing guide.

- Raise zipper foot with needle still in work, pivot, and stitch remaining zipper tape through all thicknesses to end.

- To finish, bring thread ends across bottom of placket to inside and secure. Remove original basting along seam line and press, following instructions for pressing plackets in *chapter 7 (page 151)*.

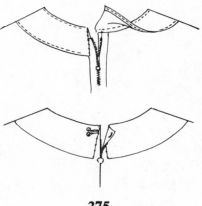

To finish a facing after a lapped zipper has been applied, turn in the end of the facing on narrow or double-stitched side of zipper and hem. On lapped side of zipper, trim off seam allowance to within ½" of neck or waistline edge. Turn facing down over zipper and mark the point where the zipper stops. Clip from edge of facing diagonally up to marked point. Turn under facing edges so they clear top of zipper and side. Hem and finish with hook-and-eye closing.

To Apply a Lapped Zipper in a Dress Placket:

- Follow all foregoing instructions for lapped zipper in skirt application. However, pivot once more across top of zipper, stitching across to meet line of top-stitching. As you stitch across, make sure zipper tab is down and pleat in seam allowance is maintained.

CHAPTER 9

Step Up to Tailoring

Tailoring is *not* for the beginning sewer!

If that bald statement of fact makes you think twice, all to the good. Tailoring may not be for the beginner, but it is certainly *not* beyond the reach of a sewer with some degree of experience—if she is willing to expend a reasonable amount of time and effort, and if she is willing to master the additional hand-sewing and pressing techniques necessary.

Tailoring—What Makes It Special?

Like so many other women, you have probably found yourself admiring a well-tailored suit or coat in a shop window or being worn with pride by another woman.

The next time you go shopping, take a closer look at the features that make a well-tailored fashion just that. You'll notice . . .

- that seams are flat and straight, without dimples or puckers;

278

- that seam edges are thin and trim, even in places where you'd expect to find bulk;

- that the lapels lie just so, yet with a shapely roll away from the neckline;

- that pockets and flaps and other construction details are crisp and precision-perfect;

- that buttonholes are beautifully made and buttons are sewed with secure shanks;

- that the collar, if there is one, rolls perfectly up and away from the neck;

- that the overall look is one of impeccable workmanship.

And if you could look inside, between lining and outer shell, you'd see a wealth of hand-stitched details molding and shaping the garment with the same loving care that tailored the outside.

So tailoring is, in essence, a building, shaping, molding process. And most of the building, shaping, and molding comes from hand-stitching and expert pressing.

Tailoring Extras—the Pressers

Since pressing is such an important part of the tailoring process, you'll need the usual pressing necessaries *plus* these indispensable extras:

- a *tailor's ham*—a firm, ham-shaped cushion that slips under curved details to facilitate pressing;

- a *press mitt*—a small pocketed and padded pressing aid that slips over the hand. Both press mitts and tailor's hams are available commercially, but they can be made quickly and inexpensively with firm cotton and a well-packed stuffing of kapok, sawdust, or wool scraps;

- a *seam roll*—a rolled, padded cushion that slips under the seam to be pressed and prevents ridges from forming;

- a *point presser*—a thin, shaped wooden board with a sharp point that helps to open seams in corners, points, and other difficult areas;

- a *wooden clapper*—a shaped wooden block that is used to pound flat a seam or edge;

- a *heavy tailor's flatiron*—a heavyweight iron that helps to produce the sharp edges so necessary in tailoring;

- *plus* the standard pressing equipment you need for regular fashion construction *(see chapter 7).*

The First Decisions—Pattern and Fabric

Everything you know about pattern and fabric selection must be put to good use now—if your venture into tailoring is to be successful.

Select a pattern that is, first of all, flattering to you. You might wish to review *chapter 1* to make sure your pattern creates the fashion illusion you want.

Then evaluate your sewing abilities honestly and select a style with classic lines and construction details you're quite sure you can handle.

Fabric selection comes next and, again, your own expertise should be one of the deciding factors. A medium-weight wool with a spongy texture and an unfinished or napped surface—like tweed or flannel—is an ideal choice if this is your first attempt at tailoring. Hard-finish wools that are difficult to shrink and press or patterned wools that need to be precisely matched are choices for the more experienced.

 **HAM**

 **MITT**

 **SEAM ROLL**

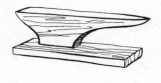 **POINT**

 **CLAPPER**

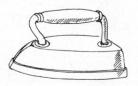

You'll also need to give more than the usual thought to your lining and interfacing selections. Linings in tailored fashions must stand up to a great deal of wear and tear. And interfacing is a key ingredient in the shaping of a tailored garment. For tips on selecting the proper lining and interlining, see *chapter 4, page 94,* and the selection chart on *page 96.*

Careful Preparation—the Key to Perfect Tailoring

Once pattern, fabrics, and notions have been selected, it's time to get to work.

Check the pattern measurements against your own—*see*

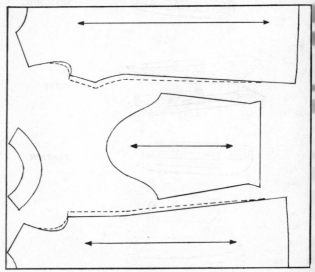

he Fashion Measurement Chart on *page 22*—and make all
the necessary pattern alterations, just as you do for a dress
or skirt.

If you are in doubt about any of your pattern alterations, you might want to make up the pattern first in
muslin—a wise idea, considering the fact that the fabric
you've selected is probably quite expensive and a sizing
mistake can be a very costly one.

Remember, of course, that muslin does not have the
fluid draping qualities of your fabric—and some additional
minor adjustments may be necessary later on. And *do*
allow sufficient ease in the muslin for the addition of
interfacing and lining that will be part of your finished
garment.

Pattern alterations for specific figure problems are detailed in *chapter 3*.

Once your pattern is prepared, it's time to turn to your
fabric. And here, too, careful preparation is a must.

Your fabrics must be preshrunk and absolutely grain-
perfect if they are to be properly molded and shaped.

Check back over *chapter 6* for information about preshrinking and achieving perfect grain lines.

It's Time to Cut

When your pattern and fabric preparations are completed
—as accurately and perfectly as you can make them—it's
time to cut your tailored fashion.

You'll find helpful information for cutting and marking
your pattern in *chapter 6*. And you'll find the following
suggestions helpful, too:

- Always cut your fashion fabric first.

- Cut seam allowances at least 1" wide—wider than
  those called for by the pattern—on all edges that might
  require fitting, like the bust, waist, and hips.

- Transfer all markings carefully if you do not plan to use an underlining. If an underlining is going to be used, transfer only the center markings to your fashion fabric, and the placement of any trims. (Grain lines should be marked on all fashion fabrics as a matter of course.)

- Cut the underlining next, if one is to be used. Transfer all seam lines, construction lines, grain lines, and marking symbols to the underlining.

- Cut the interfacing next. Most patterns have separate pattern pieces for interfacing sections. But if your pattern does not, you can make them from your jacket pattern pieces. *See below.*

- Cut the lining next. It is always advisable to cut a skirt lining for a tailored suit, whether the pattern calls for it or not. *See* **LINING,** *chapter 8,* for instructions on cutting a skirt lining.

- When all pattern pieces are cut, store them together on a flat surface until they are needed.

To cut an interfacing from a jacket pattern, mark the cutting lines on the pattern front and back as follows:

- *For the front interfacing,* mark the desired width across the hemline on the front edge. Mark at a point 3" below the armhole. Then draw a curved line from the armhole marking around and down to the hemline marking.

- *For the back interfacing,* mark at a point 3" below the armhole. Mark at a point 4" to 5" below the center back neckline. Then draw a curved line from under-arm marking to center back marking.

Cut the interfacing on the same grain line as the fashion fabric, using these markings.

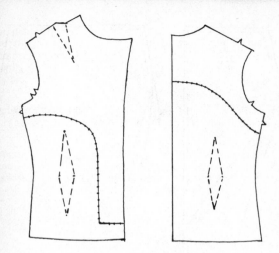

Construction Begins—Skirt First

Since all tailored garments must move easily over each
ther, the skirt must be constructed first if you are making
 suit. And after the skirt is completed, always wear it
ach time you try on the jacket.

Follow your pattern sewing guide for skirt construction
nformation. For additional lining information, or if your
attern does not include a skirt lining, see **LINING,** *chap-
r 8.*

Check the skirt and lining together for perfect fit. If the
it is satisfactory, go on to the waistband application—*see*
WAISTBANDS, *chapter 8,* for construction tips—and the
ipper application—*see* **ZIPPERS,** *chapter 8.* For an ele-
ant hand-finished look, use a hand prickstitch (*see* **HAND
STITCHES,** *chapter 8*) instead of a machine stitch on the
op side of the zipper placket.

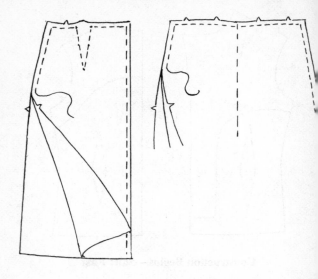

Pin up skirt and lining hems after construction has been completed, but *don't* hem them—not quite yet. The skirt hems should be completed only after the jacket hems have been prepared so the two—jacket and skirt—are in proper proportion to each other.

If you are satisfied with the fit and hang of your skirt, if the construction is flat and smooth and precise, you're ready to take on the challenge of tailoring the jacket.

Tailoring Stitches—Learn Them Now

By now you're a skilled hand with hand stitches. (*See* **BASTING** and **HAND STITCHES**, *chapter 8*). But you'll need to master these basic tailoring stitches:

- The **padding stitch** is similar to the diagonal basting stitch and is used on lapels and collars to keep the interlining in place and to secure the roll line. The padding stitch begins as a diagonal basting stitch—taking a short stitch through the fabric at a right angle to the edge and forming a longer diagonal stitch on the top. But, to make the padding stitch, you continue to work back and forth, forming a herringbone design every two rows.

- The **catch stitch** is used to join interfacings at darts and collar seams because it eliminates bulk. Simply slash interfacing darts along center markings and overlap edges to the dart stitching lines. Stitch together with a small catch stitch and trim away seam allowances close to the row of stitching.

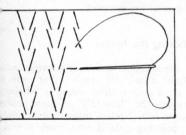

PADDING STITCH

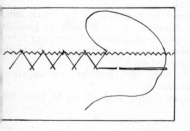

CATCH STITCH

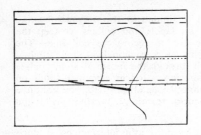

- The **tape-hemming stitch** is similar to a regular hemming stitch, except that only a thread or two is caught by the needle from the outer fabric, making the stitch invisible on the outside of the garment.

Tailoring the Jacket

Stitch all darts and construction details, following your pattern sewing guide instructions. Remember that *now* is the time to press—as each construction detail is stitched.

You might want to review the "how-to's" of construction pressing in *chapter 7, page 146*. Follow instructions closely and use the suggested pressing aids if you want a truly professional-looking finish.

Interfacing darts should be prepared by the catch stitch method *(page 287)* to eliminate as much bulk as possible.

All seam lines have been marked carefully on your fabric (or underlining) so follow them carefully as you baste the interfacing to jacket front and back.

It is wise to machine-baste the shoulder and underarm seams to get a more accurate fit.

Press these seams open lightly and go on to your first fitting.

First Fitting Checkpoints

You are trying on the shell of your jacket over the completed skirt for accurate fitting. And these are the points you'll be checking:

- That the center front markings are accurate and are positioned correctly on the body.

- That grain line markings across front and back are straight and parallel to the floor.

- That front and back darts are properly positioned.

- That all extra bulk in the darts has been removed and that dart pressing has been sharp and precise.

Sleeves and Undercollar Next

Join the sleeve seams according to your pattern directions. **SLEEVES,** *chapter 8,* offers some helpful tips for sleeve construction. Press sleeve seams open *(see chapter 7, page 150),* and hand-baste the sleeves into the armholes.

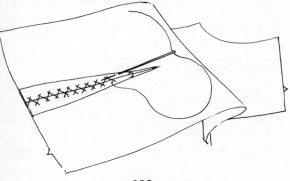

The undercollar comes next—another key step in the tailoring process.

Prepare the collar interfacing first, catch-stitching the center back sections to eliminate bulk. Then center the interfacing over the undercollar between the outer seam lines and pin in place along the neck seam line, shaping the pieces as they will be worn. The interfacing should be ⅛" short of the seam line. If it isn't, trim according to prevent bubbling later on when the seams are pressed open.

Baste the interfacing to the undercollar and *pin* the undercollar to the garment by *overlapping* seam allowances at neck edge. Now you're ready for your next fitting.

Second Fitting Checkpoints

You are trying on your jacket—over the skirt, of course —to check the following points:

- That the sleeve is properly set in the armhole.

- That sleeve grain line markings are straight and perpendicular to the floor.

- That sleeve cap grain lines are straight and parallel to the floor.

- That shoulder seams lie smoothly across the top of the shoulder.

- That the collar fits properly at the neckline; not too close to the neck and not too far away.

- That the collar roll is smooth, even, and unbroken from front to back.

- That the points of the collar and lapels rest evenly against the garment.

- That the buttonhole markings are accurately placed.

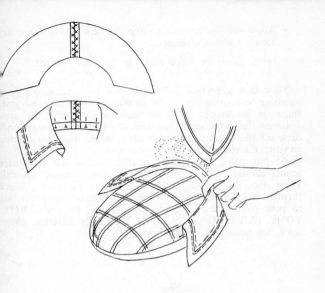

Move On to Collar and Lapels

When you are satisfied with the fit and roll of the under-collar, thread-trace the roll line and remove the undercol-lar from the jacket neck edge.

With great care—and the help of your tailor's ham and a steam iron—stabilize the roll like this:

- Pin the undercollar to the ham.

- Using steam, hold the iron *over* the roll, never *on* it, and shape the roll with your fingers working from the center back along each half to center front.

- Allow the undercollar to dry completely when you ar[e] satisfied with the shape.

- Next, shape the jacket lapels in the same manner.

Now that a perfect collar roll has been achieved, pad[-] stitching will maintain it. With the undercollar over you[r] finger in its shaped position, begin pad-stitching the are[a] between the neck seam line and the roll line. Small pad[-] ding stitches work best in this area; larger ones are neede[d] to stitch the rest of the undercollar area.

At this point, the jacket shoulder seams and underarm[m] seams should be stitched, trimmed, and pressed. At thi[s] point, too, the jacket buttonholes should be made. Wor[k] through the fashion fabric and the interfacing accordin[g] to your pattern sewing guide instructions. Or check **BUT[-] TONS, BUTTONHOLES, AND BUTTON LOOPS,** *chap[-] ter 8,* for construction information.

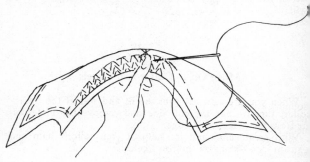

Pad-Stitch the Lapels

After the buttonholes have been completed, the next ste[p] is to pad-stitch the lapels. Start at the roll line, using th[e] same technique you used for the undercollar. Work wit[h] the interfacing side up, as you did for the undercollar, and

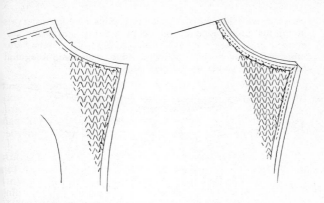

work the padding stitches in parallel rows about ½″ apart. Be careful to catch only a single thread of the shell fabric with each padding stitch. End pad-stitching at the lapel seam line.

Taping—the Stabilizing Touch

"Tape every edge that takes strain during wearing or cleaning," says the tailoring expert. And the advice is sound. Taping is a must along the front edges of a tailored jacket or coat and certainly won't hurt around armhole or neck edges.

Ribbon seam binding and cotton twill tape, ¼″ wide, are superior taping materials for tailoring. Just make sure that both are preshrunk before using.

To tape the front edges, trim away interfacing seam allowance and apply tape with a tape-hemming stitch *(see page 288).*

To tape curved edges such as the neck and armholes, use ribbon seam binding in preference to twill tape, because it adds less bulk. Make tiny clips at even intervals along the outer edge of the seam binding and place unclipped edge over the seam line. Apply with a tape-hemming stitch over the unclipped edge and long, diagonal tacking stitches over the clipped edge.

Attaching the Undercollar—the Vital Step

No step in the tailoring process is more important than the perfect positioning and attachment of the undercollar.

Pin the undercollar to the jacket, right sides together, matching markings precisely. Baste; then try on jacket to make sure the collar fits properly.

When you are satisfied with the fit of the collar, stitch. Trim interfacing seam allowance close to the stitching line at the neck. Trim fabric seam allowances and clip at evenly spaced intervals so they lie flat when pressed. Press the seam open over a tailor's ham to retain its shape.

Upper Collar and Facings Next

Join back facing to front facings at the shoulder seams and stitch upper collar to facing at neckline. Trim seam allowances and clip neckline seam allowances at evenly spaced intervals as you did with undercollar. Press seams open.

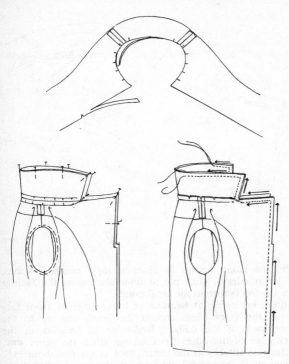

Place the upper collar and facings over the jacket, right
sides together. Work from the upper collar side, keeping
seam edges even. Pin collars together at center, points, and
notches. Match seams carefully where the undercollar joins
the jacket and the upper collar joins the front facing. Then
pin at intervals, easing the upper collar to the undercollar
and front facings to lapels. This slight easing permits collar
and lapels to roll and lie smoothly.

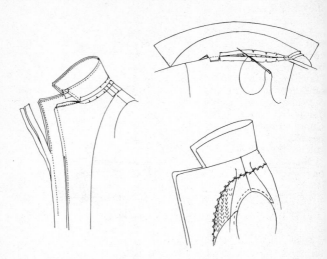

Pin the front facings in place at lapel points, notches, and lower edges. Then pin at intervals, easing the facings from the top button to the lapel points.

Stitch, beginning at hemline at lower edge of front facing, up the front edge, around the lapel, and up to the center back of the collar. Beginning at hemline at the lower edge of the other front facing, stitch the same way, overlapping stitches at the center back collar for about ½". As you stitch, be careful not to catch the tape in the seams.

If you have ever graded seams carefully (*see* **SEAMS AND SEAM FINISHES,** *chapter 8*), do so now. Even the slightest extra bulk will mar your tailoring. Trim the seam allowance of the front facings narrower than the shell fabric as far as the lapel roll line. Then reverse, trimming shell fabric closest to stitching from the roll line to the roll line on the opposite side. This will put the wider seam allowance nearest to the outside and will prevent ridges from showing. Trim diagonally across lapel point, and clip seam allowance at the point where collar and lapel meet.

Press seams open first to form flat, smooth edges. Use that handy aid, the point presser, to open seams in difficult corners. Turn the facing to the inside. Using silk thread, baste as you roll the seam edges slightly to the inside. This "favoring" prevents the seam edges from being seen on the outside of the garment.

With basting stitches holding seam edges, press with a damp cloth, using a wooden clapper to pound seams flat. Continue pressing until the crease line along the edge has been firmly set. Then, and only then, should the basting stitches be removed.

Next comes a final pressing to remove the marks of the basting stitches.

Finishing the Outer Shell

Slipstitch the back neckline seam allowances together and baste the facing to the interfacing. Tack the facing to the interfacing with invisible stitching, stopping about 5″ from the lower edges.

Now is the time to finish the underside of the button-holes. Follow your pattern sewing guide, or *see* **BUT-TONS, BUTTONHOLES, AND BUTTON LOOPS,** *chapter 8,* for instructions.

Any applied construction details—pockets, flaps, welts—come next. Make sure that these details are properly positioned, especially if you have made any alterations in your pattern. Your pattern sewing guide will have complete construction information, or *see* **POCKETS,** *chapter 8.*

You have already prepared your sleeves and basted them into your garment for your second fitting. It's time to reset your sleeves into the armholes. This, too, is a most important step, and time should be taken to make sure the sleeve cap has been properly eased and that its shape has been set by careful pressing. *See chapter 7, page 150, for* sleeve-pressing details.

Follow your pattern sewing guide for the "how-to's" of setting the sleeve into the armhole properly, or *see* **SLEEVES,** *chapter 8.*

With the sleeves basted in place, try on the shell again, checking:

- that sleeve grain line markings are straight and perpendicular to the floor;
- that sleeve caps are grain-perfect and do not wrinkle or pucker;
- that sleeve hems are marked in the right position;
- that shoulder pads, if they are to be used, do not distort the sleeve line or shoulder line;
- that jacket and skirt hems are in proportion to each other.

Stitch the sleeves and insert shoulder pads. Trim hem allowances evenly on skirt, jacket, and sleeves and baste each one at marked hemline.

Press basted hems, shrinking out any excess fullness. Prepare bias strips of interfacing (*see* **BIAS BINDING,** *chapter 8*) for jacket and sleeve hems. Cut strips ½" wider than hem allowances and the length of the edges to be hemmed plus seam allowance.

Baste interfacing strips inside hems with lower edges along the pressed hem edge and upper edges extending ½" beyond top of hem. With invisible stitching, attach bias strips to shell and attach hem to bias strips. Attach the edge of the front facing to the hem with a fine catch stitch.

A final pressing is in order now—time for all tiny creases and wrinkles to be eliminated. The importance of this pressing cannot be stressed too much. Once you line the shell, some areas will be almost impossible to press.

298

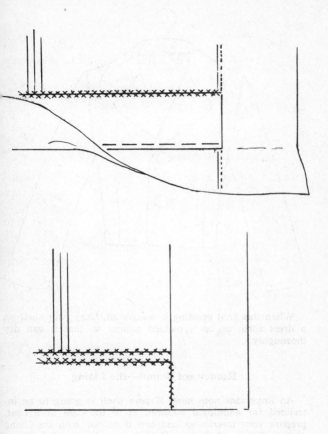

When this final pressing is completed, hang your shell on a dress form or on a padded hanger so that it can dry thoroughly.

Homeward Bound—the Lining

An important note here; if your shell is going to be interlined for additional warmth, as in the case of a coat, prepare your *interlining* and sew it as one with the lining pieces. Stitch all darts and seams, and stay-stitch front, shoulder, and neck edges. After stay-stitching lining and

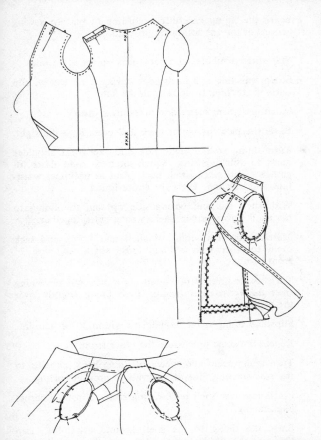

interlining together, trim away interlining close to stitching and along seams, and handle both as one construction unit.

Prepare the lining carefully according to pattern sewing instructions or use the following procedure:

- Stay-stitch armholes and back neck on the seam line.

- Stitch waistline and back neck darts. If necessary, clip darts to stitching to make them lie flat.

- Stitch underarm seams and press them open.

- Baste the pleat in center back and press it to the right.

- Turn lining to the right side and lap front shoulder darts to stitching line. Catch-stitch to hold darts together. Also catch-stitch back pleat at neckline, waistline, and hemline. Press the entire lining.

- With shell flat and wrong side up, pin the lining to the shell down center back, wrong sides together.

- Match underarm seams of shell and lining and tack them together with a long, loose stitch, stopping 3" from hemline.

- Turn under lining front seam allowance and pin lining over the front shell facing. Ease lining slightly over the bustline.

- Slipstitch lining from shoulder to within 3" of hemline.

- Repeat the same process on the other front.

- Turn under seam allowances of lining back, clipping to the stay-stitching line at intervals to prevent curling.

- Pin lining over shell back facing edge. Slipstitch across back facing.

- Baste the lining to the shell around armholes. Lap lining at shoulder seam, turning under seam allowance. Slipstitch in place.

To Apply the Sleeve Lining:

- Prepare sleeve lining as you prepared the shell sleeves, stitching underarm seams and machine-gathering the lining cap.

- Stay-stitch the underarm section of the lining between notches.

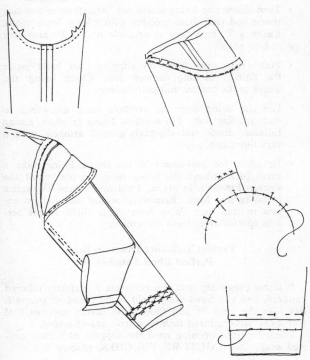

303

- Prepare the sleeve cap carefully, shaping it as you did the shell sleeve cap. Shrink out all excess ease now since this part of the garment should not be pressed again.

- Turn under the seam allowance around the sleeve cap. Clip the underarm section to stitch line so it will lie flat.

- Turn sleeve and lining inside out. Match corresponding seams and tack them together with a long, loose stitch. Leave a 2" area free at armhole and a 3" area free at hem edge.

- Turn lining over sleeve by slipping your hand inside the lining, reaching through top. Catch lining and sleeve at the bottom and pull through.

- Lap the lining over the armhole seam allowance to stay-stitching line. Pin armhole lining in place, easing fullness. Baste and slipstitch around armhole with a very tiny stitch.

- To allow for movement in the sleeve lining, take a small tuck around the lining near the bottom of the sleeve. Pin tuck in place. Fold under hem allowance in lining and hem. Remove pins and allow slight excess to fold over lining hem. This slight excess permits comfortable sleeve movement.

Perfect Tailoring Deserves the Perfect Final Touches

It is not every day that you complete a perfectly tailored garment, and you have every right to be proud of yourself. But take the time to add those little luxury touches that will make your tailored fashion a true one-of-a-kind.

Does the front opening need the support of a little covered snap? *See* **COUTURE TOUCHES,** *chapter 8.*

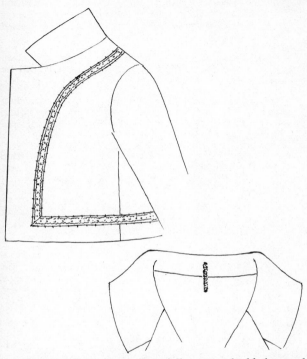

Would an inside snap, especially on a double-breasted fashion, help to keep the underlap in place? Add it.

How about a delicate, hand-applied braid where lining meets facing? Or a thread loop at the back of the neck to secure the scarf or ascot you'd like to wear? Now that you've stepped up to tailoring, you deserve these custom luxuries—and the admiring glances you're going to get when you wear your perfectly tailored fashion!

Index

312

How to Order
Extra Copies of This Book

This book is one of a series of books which make up the complete *Instant Reference Library*. Titles currently included in the series are as follows. Other titles will be added from time to time.

Instant Spelling Dictionary
Instant English Handbook
Instant Quotation Dictionary
Instant Synonyms and Antonyms
Instant Medical Spelling Dictionary
Instant World Atlas
Instant Business Dictionary
Instant Medical Adviser
Instant Secretary's Handbook
Instant Sewing Handbook
Instant Home Repair Handbook

You may order any of the above books from your local bookstore, or send your order directly to Career Institute, Dept. 899-66, 555 East Lange Street, Mundelein, Illinois 60060. Individuals, send check or money order. No COD's. Business firms or other organizations with established credit may send purchase order and be billed after delivery. The books are available in either an attractive clothbound edition at $2.25 or a deluxe leatherette, gold-stamped edition at $2.95, less the following quantity discounts:

Quantity	Discount
1 to 5 books	None
6 to 15 books	15¢ per book
16 to 49 books	25¢ per book
50 to 149 books	35¢ per book

Orders for different titles may be combined to take advantage of the above quantity prices. On orders for three or less, add 25 cents for postage and handling. Please specify whether you wish the "Cloth" or "Deluxe" binding. Illinois residents add 5% Sales Tax.